SUPER SCIENCE
⚙ EXPERIMENTS ⚙
BUILD IT

ELIZABETH
SNOKE HARRIS

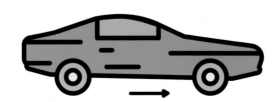

Brimming with creative inspiration, how-to projects, and useful
information to enrich your everyday life, Quarto Knows is a favorite
destination for those pursuing their interests and passions. Visit our
site and dig deeper with our books into your area of interest:
Quarto Creates, Quarto Cooks, Quarto Homes, Quarto Lives,
Quarto Drives, Quarto Explores, Quarto Gifts, or Quarto Kids.

© 2017 Quarto Publishing Group USA Inc.
Text © 2017 Elizabeth Snoke Harris

Published in 2020 by MoonDance Press, an imprint of The Quarto Group.
26391 Crown Valley Parkway, Suite 220, Mission Viejo, CA 92691, USA.
T (949) 380-7510 F (949) 380-7575 www.QuartoKnows.com

MoonDance Press titles are also available at discount for retail, wholesale,
promotional, and bulk purchase. For details, contact the Special Sales Manager by
email at specialsales@quarto.com or by mail at The Quarto Group, Attn: Special Sales
Manager, 100 Cummings Center, Suite 265D, Beverly, MA 01915, USA.

ISBN: 978-1-63322-876-4

Digital edition published in 2020
eISBN: 978-1-63322-877-1

Illustrations by Jeff Albrecht Studios

Printed in China
10 9 8 7 6 5 4 3 2

Contents

Introduction

Have you ever wanted to...
Make a mummy?
Send your own homemade rocket sky high?
Rig a fruit-powered battery?

Great! You'll find easy-to-follow instructions for these and so many more awesome at-home experiments in this book. Whether you explore friction or homemade racers, you are guaranteed to have fun!

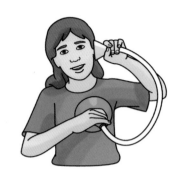

Make a Stethoscope, page 9

What's in this book?

- Many of the experiments can be done by kids all by themselves. That's right—no adult help needed. That means no grown-ups doing all the fun stuff while you watch. You can do lots of messy, cool, mind-blowing experiments all by yourself!

- All the supplies you need are probably already in your home. No fancy gadgets or doohickeys needed.

- Science is fun! There is no better boredom buster than a science experiment. You will learn something and astound and amaze your friends and family.

What are you waiting for?

Pick an experiment you are interested in, gather the materials, and get going! Make sure you check the safety instructions and find an adult to help if needed.

- **Supplies** includes all the stuff you need.

- **Do It!** has instructions for building and performing the experiment.

- **What's Happening?** Read the science behind the experiment.

- **What If?** includes ideas for making the experiment bigger, louder, longer, or just plain better.

Make It

Build contraptions that shoot, fly, roll, light up, tell time, and more!

Make Bricks

For 9,000 years, bricks have been the go-to building material. They are strong, fireproof, and waterproof. You can easily make your own mud bricks at home!

Supplies

Ice cube tray or egg carton, Bucket, Trowel, A place to dig in the ground, Straw or grass, Water

DO IT!

1. Using the trowel, dig a hole in the ground (ask your parents to help pick a spot), digging down past the dark brown topsoil to the heavier soil underneath. Does the color of the soil change as you dig deeper?

2. Put several trowels full of the deeper soil into the bucket and add a big handful of straw or grass.

3. Pour in just enough water to make a very thick mud.

4. Mix the mud and grass completely with the trowel, making sure there are no clumps or rocks in the mud.

5. Pack the mud into the ice cube tray to make small bricks, making sure there are no air bubbles by slamming the tray straight down on the ground a few times.

6. Leave the tray in a bright, dry spot for several days until the bricks are completely dry.

7. Pull the bricks out of the tray and let them dry in the sun for a few more hours.

8. Once the bricks are done, take a look at the outsides. Are they smooth or rough? Are the bricks strong or do they crumble easily? What happens if you smash one on the ground? Can you build something with your bricks?

What's Happening?

The dirt deeper in your yard usually contains a very fine, sticky soil called clay. The tiny clay particles dry into a very hard material. However, without the straw, the brick would crumble to pieces. The straw gives the brick stability and helps spread out the force on the brick to make it stronger.

What If?

What if you put more or less straw in your bricks? Does adding more straw to the bricks make them stronger?

Make a Light Bulb

The first light bulbs made by Thomas Edison were incandescent, just like this one!

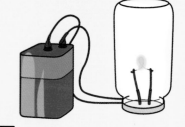

Supplies

Mason jar with lid, 1-inch nail, Hammer, Three feet of insulated copper wire, 6-volt battery (or use electrical tape to tape 4 D batteries together end to end), Picture hanging wire, Wire cutter, Stopwatch, Electrical tape

DO IT!

1. Use the hammer and nail to make two holes, 1 inch apart, in the lid of the jar.
2. Cut the copper wire into two pieces about 18 inches long.
3. With an adult's help, cut off an inch of the plastic coating at each end of the strands.
4. Push a wire through each hole so that about 2 inches of the wire can be seen in the jar.
5. Make a small hook at the end of the copper wires that will be inside the jar.
6. Unwind the picture hanging wire to use the individual fine strands of iron wire.
7. Twist three strands of the iron wire together and stretch them across the gap between the two copper hooks to form the filament.
8. Put the lid with the filament on the jar.
9. Carefully use electrical tape to attach the end of the copper wires to opposite ends of the battery. Watch your bulb light up!
10. Time how long your filament glows before it burns out. The filament becomes very hot! Wait five minutes for the filament to cool before opening the light bulb jar.

What's Happening?

The electric light bulb works because you've made a complete circuit with electrons flowing out from the battery, through the filament, and back to the battery. Electrons flowing through the filament wire produce heat and make the filament glow.

Make a Chair

Become a structural engineer!

DO IT!

Supplies

A LOT of newspaper, Tape

1. Roll several layers of newspapers into very tight rolls and secure them with tape.
2. Arrange the newspaper rolls to create a chair; tape the rolls together.
3. Sit down on your chair. Does it hold you up?
4. Experiment with different shapes like squares, triangles, and hexagons.

What's Happening?

Structural engineers call the weight an object has to hold "the load." Some shapes are better at bearing a load. Rectangles and squares are easy to bend and break. Triangles are less likely to bend or break.

Make a Dam

Dams stop or slow the flow of a river or stream and are built by people and beavers alike.

Supplies

Large, long, shallow container (large baking dish or plastic container); Sticks (from the outdoors or Popsicle sticks); Small rocks; Sand; Mud; Bucket of water

DO IT!

1. Fill the container with sand and make a path for a river.
2. Use the sticks, rocks, sand, and mud to build a dam in the middle of the container to block the river.
3. See if you can keep the area behind the dam completely dry.
4. When you're ready, slowly pour the water from the bucket into the container and see if the dam holds.

What's Happening?

When building a dam, you need to consider the materials and the shape of the dam. Sticks and rocks are strong but will not hold the water back alone. Mud and sand are needed to keep the water from leaking through the cracks.

Make Modeling Clay

Use your homemade modeling clay to create models of your favorite scientific discoveries!

DO IT!

1. Mix 2 cups of flour, 1 cup of salt, and ¼ cup of cornstarch in the bowl.
2. Mix in ¼ cup of the white glue.
3. Add water slowly, a couple spoonfuls at a time, until the clay is moldable but not too soft.
4. If you accidentally add too much water, add more cornstarch to the mixture. If the clay is too crumbly, add more glue.
5. Use your modeling clay to make whatever you like — a bowl, necklace, or model of your favorite scientific discovery. Make sure not to make pieces that are too thick (they will take too long to dry) or too thin (they will break easily). When you are ready, leave your piece in a warm, dry place to dry for two to three days.

Supplies

White school glue, Cornstarch, Flour, Salt, Water, Measuring cup, Bowl, Mixing spoon

What's Happening?

This clay is a polymer clay. The cornstarch and glue mix together to form long chains of molecules called polymers. This gives the clay its stretchiness. The flour and salt help the clay hold its shape while you work with the clay and when it dries.

Make Paper

ADULT NEEDED

Paper is the easiest product to recycle—so easy that you can recycle it into new paper at home!

Supplies

Picture frame (one that is not going to be used again), Pantyhose (a pair that is not going to be used again), Tape, Newspaper, Large bowl or bucket, Sink, Warm water, Cornstarch, Measuring spoon, Clean cloth rags or paper towels, Spoon

DO IT!

1. Remove the glass and picture from the picture frame.
2. Use the empty rectangular piece to make a strainer by stretching pantyhose over the frame, using tape if needed to hold the hose in place.
3. Tear up about six pages of newspaper into small pieces and put them into the bowl.
4. Pour warm water into the bowl to completely cover the paper, and then mix it all up.
5. Let the bowl sit for several hours or overnight, until the bowl is full of pulpy, mushy soup.
6. Mix in 2 tablespoons of cornstarch and another cup of hot water.
7. Place the frame in the sink and pour a thin layer of pulp from the bowl onto the frame.
8. Use the spoon to make sure the frame is covered evenly with pulp and to push out extra water.
9. Lay the frame on top of a dry cloth and press another cloth on top of the pulp to soak up any extra water.
10. Remove the cloth and leave the frame of pulp to dry into paper. This can take several hours, but you can use a hair dryer to speed up the process.
11. When the paper is completely dry, gently peel it off the frame. How does the paper look and feel? Can you write on it?

What's Happening?

All paper is made of millions of thin cellulose fibers from plants. When you tear the newspaper, look closely at the edges and you can see the cellulose fibers all tangled up. The fibers naturally stick together, but water breaks them apart.

Soaking the paper in water creates a cellulose pulp soup that can be made into new paper. The cornstarch helps the fibers stick back together once the water has been dried out of the pulp. A new piece of paper is born!

What If?

What if you add other items to your paper to make it more interesting? Try glitter, flower petals, or tiny pieces of colored paper.

Make a Stethoscope

The very first stethoscope was simply a hollow cylinder. Now you can make your own!

Supplies

Small funnel, Large funnel, 2 feet of plastic tubing (a piece of old water hose works too), Duct tape, Balloon, Rubber band, Scissors

 **DO IT!**

1. Blow up the balloon, let the air out, and then cut off the small end of the balloon.
2. Stretch the balloon over the large funnel, and use the rubber band to hold it in place.
3. Attach a funnel to each end of the tubing. If the funnels do not fit tightly on their own, use duct tape to secure them in place.
4. Place the small funnel on one ear and the large funnel with the balloon on your chest. Can you hear your heart beat? If not, make sure the funnel is under your shirt and move it around slowly until you can.
5. Do jumping jacks for 30 seconds and then listen to your heart beat again. Has it changed?

What's Happening?

The funnels on either end of the tube focus the sound of your heartbeat through the tube and to your ears. The balloon amplifies the vibrations of the very weak sound so that it's easier to hear. When you exercise, oxygen and nutrients are used up more quickly, so the heart needs to beat faster to send the blood through more quickly.

Make a Cantilever

A cantilever is an overhanging structure that is supported on just one end, such as a balcony or a diving board.

DO IT!

Supplies

1 package of uncooked spaghetti, Masking tape, Tabletop, Scissors, Ruler

1. Tape a small handful of pasta together and then to the top edge of the tabletop, extending out.
2. Tape another handful of pasta together and then to the bottom edge of the tabletop, using tape to secure it to the previous bunch.
3. Now add another bunch of pasta to the end, using tape to secure it to the previous bunch.
4. Keep building with more pasta and tape, extending your cantilever as far off the table as possible without getting closer than 12 inches to the ground.
5. Measure your cantilever. How long can you build it?

What's Happening?

Consider a cantilever found in nature: a tree branch. A squirrel sits on a branch near the trunk. As she runs to the end of the branch, it begins to bend. Torque, or rotation caused by a force, makes the branch bend. Torque increases farther from the support, bending the branch and cantilever down.

Make a Mummy

Egyptians weren't the only peoples to mummify their dead rulers. Mummies have been found in China, Mexico, Peru, and Chile. You can make your own mummy using an apple!

Supplies

Apple, Knife, 2 plastic cups, Washing soda (found in the detergent aisle) or baking soda, Salt, Bowl, Kitchen scale, Measuring cup, Marker, Paper towels (optional), Glue (optional)

DO IT!

1. Cut the apple into quarters and put two of the pieces into the two cups.
2. Weigh each cup on the kitchen scale and write the starting weight on the cup.
3. In the bowl, mix 1 cup of washing soda with ¼ cup of salt, then pour the mixture into one of the cups so it completely covers the apple.
4. Leave the other apple in the cup and put the cups in a cool, dry place for seven days.
5. Remove the apple pieces from the cups and inspect them. How does the apple being mummified compare to the other apple?
6. Weigh the apples in the empty cups and write the new weights on the cups.
7. Mix another batch of washing soda and salt and cover the apple again. Let the cups sit in a cool, dry place for another seven days.
8. Again, inspect the apples. How do the apples look different from one week ago? How do they look different from two weeks ago? How do they look different from each other?
9. Weigh the apples again. How much weight has each lost?
10. If you want to finish the mummifying process, dip strips of paper towel in white glue and wrap them around the mummified apple slice. Let the mummy wrappings dry for 24 hours before handling.

What's Happening?

The washing soda and salt mixture acts as a desiccant. It absorbs water and dries out the apple. Without water, bacteria and mold that cause the apple to rot can't grow. Wrapping the mummy in bandages and sealing it with glue protects the dried-out mummy from damp and dirt.

What If?

What if you mummified an orange slice, small squash, or even a hot dog?

Make a Bridge

Have you thought much about how bridges are designed?
You can build your own out of straws and paper clips.

Supplies

Books, Ruler,
Straws, Paper
clips, Scissors,
Cup, 100
pennies (or
similar weight)

DO IT!

1. Make two piles of books about 6 inches high and place them 12 inches apart.
2. Use the straws and paper clips to build a bridge that will span the distance between the books and hold a cup full of at least 100 pennies.
3. Use different methods to connect the straws with the paper clips. You can flatten the ends and slide them into the paper clip, or link the paper clips and slide each into a straw. You can also use the scissors to cut the straws to different lengths.

What's Happening?

You probably found that the straws were not strong enough to hold the pennies if you made a beam bridge. A truss bridge is much stronger and uses lighter materials to support a heavy load. Truss bridges use triangular shapes above or below a beam bridge for added strength. The diagonal pieces distribute the weight of the bridge and the load more evenly.

Make a Lava Lamp

The original lava lamp uses wax in a liquid. You can make your own
lava lamp that creates mesmerizing bubbles without heat!

DO IT!

Supplies

Clear plastic
bottle, Water,
Vegetable oil,
Food coloring,
Effervescent
tablets

1. Pour water into the bottle until it's about a quarter full.
2. Add a few drops of food coloring and shake the bottle gently to mix the color into the water.
3. Fill the rest of the bottle with vegetable oil.
4. Break an effervescent tablet into three or four pieces and drop them into the bottle.
5. Watch the colored water bubbles rise and fall in the oil!

What's Happening?

This lava lamp uses a chemical reaction and differences in density to create its mesmerizing bubbles. The effervescent tablets contain an acid and a base in powder form. When the tablet dissolves, these chemicals produce bubbles. The less-dense oil sits on top of the denser water and slows down the bubbles as they float up to the top. The bubbles also carry some of the colored water with them. When the bubbles pop, the denser drop of water sinks back down. The colored water bubbles rise and fall, as long as you add effervescent tablets.

Make a Wave Machine

Waves take many forms. Sound waves, light waves, and mechanical waves are just a few. This wave machine is a fun and mesmerizing way to explore how waves behave!

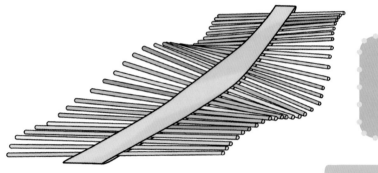

Supplies

Masking tape, 50 plastic straws, Ruler, Friend

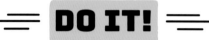

DO IT!

1. Lay 5 feet of masking tape on the ground, sticky side up.
2. Use a small piece of tape to hold each end in place, and then place straws along the entire length of the tape.
3. Leave exactly 2 centimeters between each straw and make sure the straws are centered on the tape.
4. Once all the straws are in place, lay another 5-foot-long piece of tape over the first tape to hold the straws in place.
5. Hold one end of the wave machine and have a friend hold the other (or tape it onto the back of a chair).
6. Tap one of the straws near one end. Do you see the wave travel through the straws? What happens to the wave when it reaches the end?
7. Coordinate with your friend to hit opposite ends of the wave machine at the same time. What happens to the wave? Experiment with different ways to send waves through the machine.

What's Happening?

Waves all have the same purpose: to transfer energy. In the case of the wave machine, motion energy is transferred from one end to the other by the twisting of the tape. The straws make that twisting motion more visible.

When waves collide, they travel right through each other. If the straws from one wave are down and the other straws are up, when they meet, you will see the straws stay still in that spot because the up and down motions cancel each other out.

Or if the waves in both directions are up, the motions will add together to make a larger wave at that point. The waves will also reflect or bounce back from the ends, but how they reflect depends on if the ends are loose or held in place. Try it out; what do you observe?

What If?

What if you make a wave machine with the straws spaced farther apart or closer together?

Galileo's Ball Drop

Historians are pretty sure that Galileo didn't drop a feather and a cannonball off the Leaning Tower of Pisa, but that doesn't mean you can't drop some balls off the top of a ladder.

This experiment is best done outdoors where the falling balls won't do any damage.

DO IT!

1. Set up the ladder outside, in an area where the balls will hit a hard surface (so you can use the sound of them hitting the ground to help figure out which lands first).

2. Ask your friend to hold the ladder, and then carefully climb up a few steps and hold the balls out in front of you.

3. Drop the balls at the same time, being careful not to push or throw them.

4. Listen and watch to see which ball hits the ground first. Repeat this two or more times to make sure the results are consistent. If you want, use a video camera to record the balls falling so you can watch it back and see what happened.

Supplies

2 balls that are the same size but different weights (for example a tennis ball and a field hockey ball, or a basketball and a medicine ball), Ladder, Friend

What's Happening?

When two balls of the same size but different weights fall, they accelerate or speed up at the same rate. Gravity pulls down the heavier ball with a bigger force, but the heavy ball has more mass, so it takes a bigger force to accelerate it. The lighter ball needs a smaller force to accelerate, so both balls speed up the same amount and hit the ground at the same time!

This is actually true for any object, even a feather and a cannonball, but air gets in the way. The air resistance pushing up will slow down the feather much more than the cannonball, so it appears that gravity pulls the feather less and it falls slower.

If you could remove the air, you would see the feather and bowling ball fall together.

What If?

What if you drop two balls that are the same weight but different sizes or shapes?

Fun Fact
Galileo actually did his experiments by sliding objects down a ramp so they moved slower and could be timed with a water clock—there were no digital stopwatches or smartphones then!

Double Ball Drop

A ball bouncing on the ground is nothing special, but when you put one ball on top of another ball and let them bounce together, something surprising happens!

This experiment is best done outside on concrete or another hard, flat surface.

Supplies

Large ball (basketball, soccer ball, or similar size), Smaller ball (tennis ball or similar size)

What's Happening?

When you hold the ball out, ready to drop, the ball has potential or stored energy. When you release the ball, gravity pulls it downward, turning that stored energy into motion, or kinetic energy. When the large ball hits the ground, it compresses or squishes, and its motion energy gets stored as elastic energy, like a spring. As the ball releases, it pushes up on the small ball on top, passing on that stored elastic energy.

Why does the small ball go SO high? The small ball has much less mass than the large ball so that extra energy causes it to go even faster than the large ball, which means it bounces much higher than it would on its own.

DO IT!

1. Hold the large ball out at shoulder height and drop it. How high does it bounce?
2. Hold the small ball out at shoulder height. How high does this ball bounce?
3. Now place the small ball directly on top of the large ball.
4. Hold them out at shoulder height and drop them together. Now how high do the balls bounce?

The Way the Ball Bounces

If you've ever played a ball sport when it's very cold outside, you may have noticed that the balls don't bounce as high or travel as far as when it's warmer. Find out why!

This experiment is best done outside on concrete or another hard, flat surface.

Supplies

6 golf balls, Yardstick, Freezer, Friend

What's Happening?

The bounciness of a ball depends on its elasticity, and a golf ball is fairly elastic. When you hit the ball with a golf club, most of that energy goes into the motion of the ball. However, if you freeze the golf ball, it becomes more rigid and brittle, and less elastic. The ball doesn't squish as much when it hits the ground, so less energy goes into the bounce and the ball doesn't get as high as a warmer, more elastic ball.

DO IT!

1. Put three golf balls in the freezer for at least two hours and leave the other three out at room temperature.
2. Have a friend hold the yardstick straight up from the ground.
3. Drop the balls one at a time from the top of the yardstick, and make a note of how high each of the balls bounces. Which ball bounced higher: the frozen golf balls or the room-temperature balls?

Racquetball Popper

Cut open a rubber ball to make a popping fun toy!

Supplies

Racquetball (or another hollow rubber ball), Scissors, Table tennis ball

1. Use the scissors to cut the racquetball in half down the middle.
2. Choose a side without any tears or trim the tears off.
3. Trim off about ¼ inch so the popper is slightly less than half a ball.
4. Hold the sides and push the middle out so the popper is inside out; you may need to squeeze the sides together a few times to get it to stay inside out.
5. Hold the popper, curved side up, out in front of you and drop it on the ground. The popper will "pop" when it hits the ground and bounce up higher than it was dropped from!
6. Turn the popper inside out again, then turn it upside down so the curved side is down and place the table tennis ball in the popper cup.
7. Drop the popper and watch the ball shoot up!

What's Happening?

Elastic energy is stored in the popper by pushing it inside out. Holding the popper out over the floor stores gravitational energy. When you drop the popper on the floor, this turns into kinetic motion energy. The release of that stored energy sends the popper into the air. When you put the ball on the popper, the same thing happens, except a table tennis ball is much lighter than the popper. So the ball shoots up even higher!

Shoot the Moon

Roll a ball all the way to the top of a hill using gravity alone.

Supplies

Table tennis ball, 2 bamboo skewers (or other long sticks), Book (about 1 inch thick), Rubber band, Bottle caps (optional)

1. Line up the two bamboo sticks next to each other and wrap the rubber band around one end to hold them together. You should be able to easily open the sticks into a V shape.
2. Lay the book on the table and place the open end of the V at the edge of the book.
3. Place the table tennis ball at the point of the V.
4. Adjust the sticks back and forth to change the shape of the V so the ball rolls uphill toward the book. Can you get the ball to roll to the book without falling through the sticks?
5. To make the game, place bottle caps in a row between the bottom point of the V and the top near the book.
6. Each cap is worth a different number of points, with the cap near the point worth the least, and near the book worth the most. Drop the ball into the bottle cap closest to the book to get the most points!

What's Happening?

The ball doesn't really roll uphill—it just looks that way! As the ball rolls, the center of the ball lowers, and it appears to roll up when actually the ball is rolling down!

15

Cradle of Energy

How does energy transfer from one object to another? You'll find out in this experiment!

Supplies

5 bouncy balls, 5 pushpins, Thread, 4 identical bottles (at least 8 inches tall), 4 bamboo skewers, Ruler, Tape

DO IT!

1. Stick a pushpin into each of the bouncy balls, then cut four pieces of thread 17 inches long.
2. Tie the center of each thread around a pushpin in the bouncy balls.
3. Fill the bottles with water and put the caps on to make them more stable.
4. Place the bottles at four corners of a rectangle that is 6 inches wide and 10 inches long.
5. Tape bamboo skewers to the lids of the bottles to hold them in place, making sure the sides of the rectangle are straight.
6. Tie the ends of the thread for each bouncy ball to the bamboo skewers on opposite long sides of the rectangle, making sure each ball hangs at the exact same height.
7. The balls should line up perfectly, hung so they are almost touching and as low as possible.
8. Use a small piece of tape to hold each string to the bamboo skewer so it doesn't slide around.
9. Pull back a ball from one end and let it go. Watch the ball on the other end fly out!
10. Try pulling back two balls and letting go. How many balls come out the other side?

What's Happening?

Whenever two objects collide, the total momentum and kinetic energy stay the same. Both of these depend on the mass and the speed of the objects that collide. So, if a fast-moving object hits an object of the exact same mass that is sitting still, the momentum and energy is transferred from the fast object to the still object.

If the collision is elastic, energy is not lost to friction, heat, sound, or anything else, and the still object will zoom off with the same speed as the fast object and the fast object will stop.

This is exactly what happens in this example, also called Newton's cradle. The balls all have the same mass, and the hard rubber makes for a mostly elastic collision.

What If?

What if you add more balls to the Newton's cradle? What if you use marbles or some other ball?

Tennis Ball Shooter

Projectile motion is the study of how objects move through the air. Make a shooter to explore how a tennis ball flies through the air—or make several and have a battle with your friends!

Supplies

Tennis ball can or cardboard tube (like a potato chip container), Plastic drink bottle that fits inside the tennis ball can, Rubber bands, Scissors, Masking tape, Pencil or skewer, Tennis ball

ADULT NEEDED

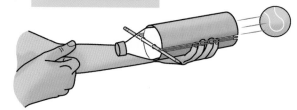

DO IT!

1. Cut the bottom off of the tennis ball can so you have a long straight tube, then cut two slits on one end of the can about ½ inch apart.
2. Cut similar slits on the opposite side of the same end of the can and hook a rubber band through the slits on each side of the can.
3. Wrap masking tape around the top of the can with the slits to hold the top of the rubber bands in place.
4. With an adult's help, use the scissors to poke a hole in the drink bottle about 2 inches from the top (where the bottle stops curving).
5. Poke another hole on the opposite side of the bottle and slide the pencil through the holes so it's evenly balanced on both sides.
6. Put the bottle into the can, bottom end first, on the side opposite the rubber bands.
7. Stretch the rubber bands and slide one over each end of the pencil.
8. Now place a tennis ball in the opposite end of the can. To shoot the ball, pull back the bottle and pencil and release! How far does the ball go?

What's Happening?

Once the ball leaves the shooter, the only force acting on it is gravity. Gravity slows any upward motion of the ball until it stops going up for just an instant and then accelerates downward. However, gravity does not affect the ball's sideways motion. The combination of the constant sideways motion and gravity pulling downward causes the ball to move in a curved path, called a parabola.

What If?

What if you use different balls in your shooter? Try table tennis balls or rubber bouncy balls. What type of ball shoots the farthest?

Popsicle Stick Catapult

Catapults have been used for centuries to hurl large rocks at enemies. This catapult hurls marshmallows!

Supplies

9 Popsicle sticks, 6 rubber bands, 1 plastic spoon, Mini marshmallows or other ammunition

1. Stack seven sticks and wrap a rubber band several times around each end to hold them tightly together.
2. Put the other two sticks together and wrap a rubber band several times around just one end.
3. Push the stack of seven sticks in between the open end of the two sticks as far as possible.
4. Use another rubber band to secure all of the sticks in place so that the rubber band makes an "X" where all the sticks meet.
5. Lay the spoon on the stick that is up in the air.
6. Use two rubber bands to secure the spoon to the stick, one near the top and another near the bottom.
7. Place a mini marshmallow in the spoon, pull the spoon down, and release. Watch the marshmallow fly!

What's Happening?

Catapults are one example of a lever. They use a beam or stick on a fulcrum, so the work done on one end is increased on the other end, making it easier to lift heavy things.

In this catapult, pulling back the spoon (lever) attached to the rubber bands (fulcrums) stores that work as potential energy. The stretched-out rubber bands store the potential energy until you release the catapult. The rubber bands then snap back into place and transfer most of the potential energy to the marshmallow as kinetic or motion energy, making your ammo fly!

Want S'more Catapult?

This catapult is a sweet treat!

Supplies

5 large marshmallows, 7 wooden skewers, Plastic spoon, Rubber band, Masking tape, Mini marshmallows

1. Place three large marshmallows in a triangle and connect them with skewers.
2. Add three more skewers and another marshmallow to form a pyramid.
3. Place the spoon handle along one end of the last skewer, and secure with tape.
4. Loop the rubber band over the top of the pyramid.
5. Slide the pointed end of the skewer with the spoon through the rubber band and down into the marshmallow on the opposite side.
6. Place a mini marshmallow into the spoon, and use one hand to hold the catapult down and the other to pull back the spoon. Release and watch the marshmallow fly!

Seed Spinners

Have you ever blown the seeds off a dandelion puff to make a wish? Did you watch the puffy white seeds float through the air? If you look carefully, you'll see that the seeds look like tiny helicopters. They are designed to float through the air for a long time to spread the dandelion seeds far and wide. Create your own spinner similar to a dandelion seed and see how long it will spin in the air!

Supplies

Paper, Ruler, Scissors, Paper clip

DO IT!

1. Cut a strip of paper about 1½ inches wide and 8½ inches long.
2. Fold the paper into thirds, crease the folds, and then unfold the paper.
3. Cut a slit from the top almost all the way to the first fold, leaving about a ½-inch between the end of the cut and the fold.
4. Cut two small ½-inch slits on both sides, right along the first fold, and then fold the paper up on the second fold.
5. Now fold the sides inward on the two small slits you cut, and fold up the bottom toward the top, securing it with a paper clip.
6. Finally, fold the top two strips in opposite directions. Your seed spinner is complete!
7. Drop your spinner high above the ground, maybe from the top of the stairs or standing on a ladder.

What's Happening?

The shape of the seed spinner causes it to start spinning around after it falls for a second or two. The spinning motion causes lift, or an upward force on the seed spinner, which slows down its fall.

In fact, lift causes the seed spinner to fall much slower than the same paper and paper clip crumpled up in a ball — try it! For seeds, this means they spend more time in the air. Any breeze or wind can carry the seeds farther away where they can take hold in the ground and grow into new plants!

What If?

What if you change the shape of the seed spinner? Try making the wings longer or shorter, folding up a corner, or making the end rounded instead of square.

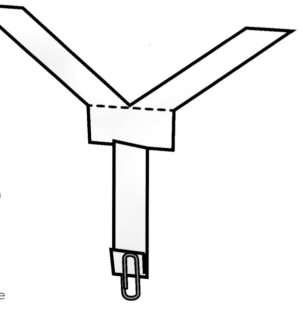

Centripetal Spinner

Once you get the hang of this little spinner, there will be no stopping you!

Supplies

Wooden skewer,
Scissors,
Tape, Cork

= DO IT! =

1. Break the wooden skewer in half, and use the scissors to cut off any splinters.
2. Tape the skewers together in an X-shape so the two sides of the X are shorter than the other two, making sure the point of the skewer is on a longer side.
3. Push the cork onto the pointy end of the skewer and then balance the spinner on your finger between the two longer sides.
4. Move your hand so that the skewers spin around your finger.
5. Once you get it moving, point your finger upward at an angle so it doesn't slide off.
6. How long can you keep the centripetal spinner twirling around your finger?

What's Happening?

Your finger pulls on the skewer, which pulls on the cork and keeps it moving in a circle. This pulling is called centripetal or "center-seeking" force and it keeps the spinner twirling around your finger instead of flying off.

Straw Spinner

You might look a little like an elephant with these straws in your mouth!

= DO IT! =

Supplies

2 bendable straws,
Aluminum foil,
Small rubber band, Scissors

1. Cut a 2-inch strip of foil and fold it so you have a piece that is 2 inches long and ½ inch wide.
2. Loosely wrap the foil strip around the short end of the straw.
3. Wrap the rubber band around the end of the straw so that the foil "bead" doesn't slide off.
4. Cut the long end of each straw in half, and then cut a 1-inch slit on the long end of one straw.
5. Squeeze that straw and slide it inside the long end of the other straw. The straws should fit together tightly but air should still flow through both straws.
6. Bend both straws so the short parts are at a right angle to the long parts.
7. Turn the straws so the bent parts are at right angles to each other, and then place the end of the straw with the foil bead in your mouth.
8. Hold the bead lightly between your lips and blow hard. The straws will spin around!

What's Happening?

Newton's third law states that for every force, there is an equal and oppositely directed re-force. In this case, the force is the air you blow. The air pushes out of the straw, so there is a re-force of the same size, but pushing the opposite direction on the straw.

Straw Propeller

This propeller won't make you fly into the air, but it's still fun to spin around.

Supplies

Drinking straw, Milkshake straw (big enough for the drinking straw to fit inside), Scissors, Tape

DO IT!

1. Fold the smaller straw 2 inches from the end and cut off one corner where the straw bends.
2. When you open the straw, there is a diamond-shaped hole; tape the end of the straw closed on the side closest to the hole.
3. Fold the larger straw in the middle and cut off both corners where it bends.
4. When you open this straw, there are two diamond-shaped holes; flatten both ends of the straw and tape them closed.
5. On the left side, cut off the top corner of the taped end to create a small hole.
6. On the right side, cut off the bottom corner of the taped end to create a small hole on the opposite side of the straw.
7. Slide the small straw through the hole in the large straw so the holes line up.
8. Put the open end of the small straw in your mouth and blow hard. The large straw will spin around like a propeller!

What's Happening?

When you blow into the small straw, there is nowhere for the air to go but out of the diamond hole and into the larger straw. From there, the air goes out the small holes on both ends of the large straw. Because the holes are on opposite corners and not the ends of the straw, the air blowing out pushes back on the straw, causing it to spin!

Pocket Slingshot

Be ready for a marshmallow battle anytime!

Supplies

Plastic drink bottle, Balloon, Scissors, Mini marshmallows

DO IT!

1. Cut the top off of the bottle just below the mouth.
2. Cut off the narrow part of the balloon, and then stretch the rest of the balloon over the mouth of the bottle, pushing it through so it folds over the opening.
3. Pull the narrow part of the balloon onto the mouth of the bottle, as well.
4. Roll up the smaller piece of balloon so that it holds the larger piece in place.
5. Put a marshmallow in the balloon, pull it back and release it. How far can you shoot the marshmallow?

What's Happening?

This slingshot shoots using the first law of thermodynamics: energy cannot be created or destroyed, only transformed. In this case, potential energy in the stretchy balloon is converted to motion energy.

Stomp Rocket

Shoot off a paper rocket with this bigger version of the squeeze rocket on page 29.

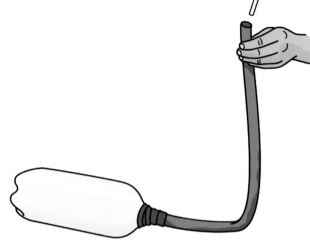

rocket on page 29.

Supplies

Empty 2-liter bottle, Bicycle inner tube, Duct tape, 2 pieces of printer paper, Scissors, Clear tape

DO IT!

Make the Launcher

1. Cut the valve off of the bicycle tube so you have a long, straight tube about 2 feet long.
2. Stretch one end of the tube over the mouth of the bottle.
3. Wrap duct tape around the tube and bottle so that it's secure and won't pop off when you stomp on the bottle.
4. Roll up one piece of paper longways as tight as you can so that you have a long, thin tube.
5. Use the clear tape to tape the paper along the length of the tube so that it stays securely in place.
6. Slide the paper tube into the end of the inner tube.
7. Use duct tape to hold it in place and seal the connection so no air can escape.

Make the Rocket

1. Cut the second piece of paper in half longways.
2. Wrap one half around the paper tube on the launcher.
3. Tape the rocket tube so it doesn't unroll and slide it off of the launcher tube.
4. Cut 2 inches off the rocket tube so that it is a bit shorter than your launcher tube.
5. Use the other half of the paper to make a nose cone and fins.
6. To make a nose cone, cut out a half circle, roll it up into a cone and tape it to the top of your rocket.
7. To make fins, cut out three triangles, and fold a tab on one side that you can tape to the rocket.
8. To launch your rocket, slide the rocket onto the launch tube. Have your friend hold the bottom of the launch tube (but not the rocket!) pointed upward. Stomp as hard as you can on the bottle and watch your rocket fly!

What's Happening?

This rocket uses Newton's first law of motion. When you stomp on the bottle, air is pushed very quickly through the tube and into your rocket, pushing it up. Because your rocket is so light, this large force on a small mass makes your rocket accelerate to a great speed. The more force you use when you stomp, the faster your rocket flies, and the higher it will go.

Underwater Volcano

ADULT NEEDED

Not all volcanoes are on mountaintops. In fact, there are millions of underwater volcanoes in oceans all over the world!

Supplies

Glass measuring cup, Small candle, Sand, Water, Stove or hot plate

DO IT!

1. Place the candle in the bottom of the cup. Carefully cover the candle with sand.
2. Pour water into the cup so that it's almost to the top.
3. Place the cup on the stove or hot plate and turn the heat on medium.
4. Watch your sand volcano erupt! (Don't forget to turn off the stove when your volcano is done.)

What's Happening?

As the wax heats up and melts, you will see a bump form in the sand layer. When the wax gets hot enough, the bump will erupt and hot wax will flow through the sand and float to the top of the water. This is exactly what happens in a real volcano. Magma from the hot core of the Earth heats up and expands so that it pushes up through the earth and becomes lava. When the lava, just like the wax, hits the water, it cools and hardens.

Ketchup Volcano

Use ketchup to make your lava and eruption look more like the real thing!

Supplies

Plastic cup; Newspaper, tape, clay and paint (optional); Baking dish; Ketchup; Baking soda; Dish soap; Bowl; Mixing spoon; Measuring spoon; Measuring cup

DO IT!

1. Use a plastic cup, newspaper, and tape to make the form for your volcano. Cover this with clay if you want.
2. Put your plastic cup volcano in a baking dish.
3. In a bowl, mix a cup (or more) of ketchup, a squirt of dish soap and ½ cup of water. Pour this into the plastic cup volcano.
4. Add 2 tablespoons of baking soda.

What's Happening?

Ketchup is made with vinegar, which reacts with the baking soda to make carbon dioxide gas. The gas gets trapped in the soap, creating a bubbly volcano!

Drink Bottle Rocket

Do this experiment outdoors, as a powerful explosion really sends this rocket flying.

Supplies

Sports bottle with pop-open cap, Ceramic mug, Effervescent tablet (such as Alka Seltzer), Water

DO IT!

1. Have an adult help you find a safe outdoor place to launch your rocket.
2. Fill the bottle about half full with warm water.
3. Put half of an effervescent tablet in the rocket, and shake it up for just two seconds. Quickly place the bottle upside down in the mug.
4. Wait. In about 10 to 30 seconds, your rocket will shoot. Warning: Do not pick up the rocket or place your face or any body part above the rocket. You could get hurt.

What's Happening?

The tablet is made of citric acid, the same acid found in lemons and oranges, and sodium bicarbonate, also known as baking soda. When these two chemicals mix in the water, they react to create carbon dioxide gas inside your rocket. As more and more gas is created, the pressure builds. When the cover can't hold anymore, it pops out and all the gas goes rushing out.

Geyser

When it comes to eruptions, volcanoes get all of the attention, but geysers can produce some pretty amazing explosions too!

Supplies

Funnel, Pot (that's as tall as the funnel), 3-foot-long plastic tubing, Water

DO IT!

1. Put the funnel in the pot with the large end facing down.
2. Fill the pot with water.
3. Slide one end of the tube under the funnel. You may need to hold the funnel down if it floats.
4. Blow into the other end of the tube, and watch the water fly up out of the geyser! How high can you make the water shoot out of the spout?

What's Happening?

Real geysers are caused by funnel-shaped cracks underground that are filled with water. When water at the bottom of the funnel gets so hot that it boils, the bubbles of steam rise to the surface and shoot out of the geyser, along with the water at the top of the funnel.

Experi-mint Explosion

You've probably shaken up a bottle of soda and opened it up to watch it spray all over the place. (And if you haven't, you should!) In this experiment, you will add mint candies to the soda for an explosion that will blow you away. This experiment is very messy and best performed outdoors.

Supplies

2-liter bottle of soda, 12 Mentos mints, Paper, Index card, Tape, Measuring cup, Rain poncho (optional)

DO IT!

1. Find an outside area to launch your rocket. Roll and tape the piece of paper into a tube about 1 inch wide. Make sure the mints fit in the tube. Slide 12 mints into the tube and put the index card under the tube so they don't fall out.

2. Do the next steps quickly to get a larger explosion. You can put the poncho on now if you are worried about getting sprayed with soda!

3. Carefully open the bottle of soda. Place the index card and tube of mints on top of the bottle opening.

4. Quickly slide out the index card so the mints drop in the soda bottle. Make a run for it or you will be covered with soda!

5. After the soda explosion, carefully pour the soda that's left in the bottle into a measuring cup. How much soda was left in the bottle?

6. A 2-liter bottle has about 8.45 cups of liquid. Subtract the amount left in the bottle from 8.45 cups to get the amount of soda that exploded out of the bottle.

What's Happening?

Soda gets its fizz from the carbon dioxide gas dissolved in the soda. When you open a bottle of soda, you can hear the fizz and see the bubbles of gas. If you shake up the bottle first, there's more fizz and bubbles because the gas is released faster. Adding the mints just makes the bubbles come out of the soda even faster. The gas comes out so fast that it takes most of the soda with it, making an awesome explosion.

If you look closely at the outside of the mints, you can see tiny little holes that feel chalky. This texture and the ingredients in the mints help break up the hold that the soda has on the carbon dioxide gas. Other flavors of mints don't work as well because they have a smooth, waxy coating that keeps them from dissolving and freeing the carbon dioxide gas.

What If?

What if you use a different type of soda? Try different flavors, including regular and diet.

Do different flavors of mints also cause explosions? Other materials give similar (or even bigger!) explosions. Try rock salt, table salt, and Wintergreen Life Savers.

Water Bottle Rocket

Pump up this rocket with a ball pump and it will fly past the treetops!
Fair warning: You're likely to get wet with this one!

Supplies

Empty 2-liter soda bottle; Cork that fits tightly in the bottle (if your cork is too small, wrap tape around it); Ball pump with a needle; Garden pitchfork, rake, or shovel with a handle; Water

═ DO IT! ═

1. With an adult's help, push the needle of the ball pump all the way through the cork so that it comes out the other end.

2. Push the rake or pitchfork into the ground so that the handle is near the ground at a slight angle. If you don't have a tool with a handle, you can use branches or something similar to make a launch pad for your rocket.

3. Fill about a quarter of the bottle with water. Seal the bottle with the cork.

4. Place your rocket on the launch pad so that the neck of the bottle goes through the handle, which supports your rocket. The cork and ball pump will be underneath the handle.

5. Carefully and steadily pump up your bottle while keeping the bottle lined up on the launch pad.

6. Keep pumping until the cork pops off and the rocket shoots into the air!

What's Happening?

As you push air into the bottle rocket with the pump, the air pressure builds up until the cork can no longer hold it in. The air and water come rushing down and the rocket goes shooting up. This demonstrates Newton's third law: every force (the air and water rushing down) has an equal and opposite force (the rocket shooting up).

Newton's second law is also at work here: acceleration equals the force divided by the mass. The bottle and water feel the same force, but because the bottle has a much smaller mass than the water and air, it has a much greater acceleration.

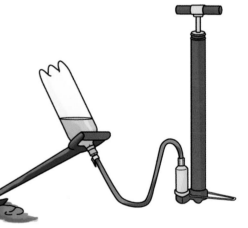

What If?

What if you add more or less water to the bottle? What is the ideal amount of water for the highest flight?

Add a nose cone and fins to your rocket to make it more aerodynamic. Does this make it fly higher? You can even add a parachute so that the rocket will stay in the air longer on the way down.

Balloon Rocket

You can launch this rocket indoors. Make two or more and have balloon rocket races with your friends!

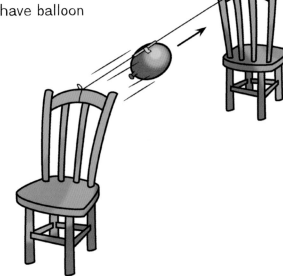

Supplies

Long piece of string (10 to 15 feet long), 2 chairs (or other objects about the same height and 10 to 15 feet apart), Straight straw, Tape, Balloons, Scissors

DO IT!

1. Tie one end of the string to one of the chairs.
2. Slide the straw onto the string, and then tie the other end to the other chair, 10 to 15 feet away. Make sure the string is taut and straight.
3. Put a piece of tape across the top of the straw.
4. Blow up one of the balloons. Hold the end closed but do not tie it off.
5. Put the balloon under the straw and use the tape to attach the balloon to the straw.
6. Slide your balloon rocket all the way to one end of the string so that the open end of the balloon is close to one of the chairs.
7. Release the balloon and watch it fly! Does it get all the way to the other chair?
8. Blow up the balloon and try again, or set up two strings and have balloon rocket races with a friend.

What's Happening?

When you blow up a balloon, you're creating a much higher air pressure inside the balloon than outside. When you release the balloon, the air rushes out and pushes the balloon in the opposite direction. If you just blow up a balloon and let it go, the balloon will fly all over the room in all directions (try it!). By attaching the balloon to the straw and string, you can control which way the air flies out of the balloon and which direction the balloon flies. The balloon rocket will keep moving until all of the air is out of the balloon.

What If?

What if you use different sizes and shapes of balloons? Use a stopwatch to see which balloon makes it to the other end of the string in the shortest amount of time.

Can your balloon rocket carry cargo? Use a cereal box to make a small, lightweight box to carry small toys or even candy from one end of the string to the other.

Lemon Juice Bottle Rocket

Ready for a rocket launch with a bang? Prepare for lift-off!

Supplies

Empty 16-ounce plastic soda or water bottle, Cork that fits tightly in the bottle (if your cork is too small, wrap tape around it), Toilet paper, Lemon juice, Baking soda, Measuring spoon, Water, Scissors, Funnel

 **DO IT!**

1. Find a place outdoors to launch your rocket.

2. Use the funnel to pour lemon juice into the bottle so that it's about an inch deep.

3. Then pour water into your bottle so that it's half full.

4. Put 1 teaspoon of baking soda into the center of a square of toilet paper.

5. Fold up the toilet paper to make a little packet.

6. Drop the baking soda packet into the bottle and close it up with the cork.

7. Shake up the bottle and stand back. Within a few seconds your cork rocket will lift off!

What's Happening?

As the water and lemon juice soak through the toilet paper, the acid in the lemon juice reacts with the baking soda to produce carbon dioxide gas. As the gas pressure builds up in the bottle, it pushes the cork out with a bang and sends it shooting into the air!

What If?

What if you use more lemon juice? Or more baking soda? Try other acids, such as soft drinks and vinegar. What if you use a different-sized bottle?

Tea Bag Rocket

ADULT NEEDED

This gentle rocket is more like a hot air balloon than a space rocket, but it's still fun to launch!

Supplies

**Tea bag,
Matches,
Ceramic plate,
Scissors**

DO IT!

1. Cut open the top of the tea bag and dump out the tea.
2. Open up the empty tea bag to a tube shape, and stand it on the ceramic plate.
3. Have an adult use the lighter to light the top of the tea bag. The bag will burn down to the bottom and then fly up into the air!

What's Happening?

When you light the tea bag at the top, it traps air inside the bag. The hot air expands so that the hot air inside the bag is less dense than the cooler air outside the bag. The more dense air outside of the bag pushes up through the bottom of the bag, causing the air inside the bag to move upward. This movement of hot and cool air is called convection. As the bag burns completely into ash, it becomes light enough to be launched upward by this air current.

Squeeze Rockets

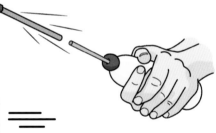

This portable rocket is powered simply by the strength of your hands!

Supplies

**Plastic bottle,
Modeling clay, 2
straws of different
sizes (one should fit
inside the other)**

DO IT!

1. Put one end of the smaller straw in the opening of the bottle so that most of the straw is out of the bottle.
2. Use a bit of the modeling clay to hold the straw in place and seal the top of the bottle.
3. Put a small piece of modeling clay in one end of the larger straw to seal it off, as well.
4. Slide the larger straw over the smaller straw and squeeze the bottle as hard and quickly as you can.

What's Happening?

This rocket makes use of Newton's first law of motion: An object will stay at rest (or moving in a straight line and constant speed) unless a force acts on it. In this case, when you squeeze the bottle, you're applying force to the bottle, which then pushes the air inside the bottle, which in turn pushes out the rocket straw.

By Land & By Air

You don't need an engineering degree to fashion fast cars and flying machines!

Mousetrap Car

ADULT NEEDED

Just add wheels to a simple mousetrap and you will be ready to roll!

Supplies

Mousetrap, String, Straw, Cardboard, Cup, Pencil, Scissors, Tape, Bamboo Skewer, Glue or clay

 **DO IT!**

1. Ask an adult to help you make sure the mousetrap is closed and not set, and remove the parts of the trap used to hold the bait (catch) and the long hook that keeps the rectangular hammer in place (catch lever).
2. Cut four pieces of straw about ½ inch long and tape them to the bottom of the mousetrap, two in the front and two in the back, near the outside edges of the mousetrap to hold the axles.
3. Make sure the pieces line up so the axles can spin freely.
4. Cut the bamboo skewer in half and put the two pieces through the straws.
5. Trace the cup four times on the piece of cardboard and cut out the circles to make wheels.
6. Use the scissors to poke a small hole in the center of the cardboard circles, and then slide the wheels onto the ends of the bamboo skewer axles.
7. Use glue or a small amount of clay to hold the axles in place on the wheels, making sure the wheels don't rub against the sides of the mousetrap.
8. Cut a piece of string about twice as long as the mousetrap, and tie one end to the middle of the skewer axle in the back of the mousetrap (farthest from the hammer).
9. Carefully tie the other end of the string to the top of the hammer, using a small bit of tape to hold both ends of the string in place.
10. With an adult's help, turn the back wheels so that the string winds tightly around the axle.
11. Lift the hammer to the other side and keep winding the string tightly.
12. Place the mousetrap car on the floor and let go of the hammer. It will slowly pull the string so that the car zooms!

What's Happening?

There is a lot of energy stored in the tight spring of a mousetrap. When you release the spring, that stored potential energy is converted into moving kinetic energy that pulls the string, which in turn pulls the axle and turns the wheels.

Balloon Car

This car uses the same science that sends rockets into space!

Supplies

Cardboard, 2 straws, 2 bamboo skewers, 4 plastic bottle caps, Clay, Balloon, Tape, Scissors, Ruler

DO IT!

1. Cut a 3" x 5" piece of cardboard.
2. Cut two 3-inch pieces from a straw.
3. For the axles, tape one straw near the front and one straw near the back so the edges of the straw line up with the edges of the cardboard.
4. Fill the bottle caps with clay and cut the pointed end off of each skewer.
5. Stick one end of each skewer into the clay at the center of a bottle cap.
6. Slide each skewer through a straw and then stick wheels on the other ends.
7. Make sure the car rolls straight; adjust the placement of the skewers in the wheels as needed.
8. Place one end of the other straw in the opening of the balloon and tape it to the end of the straw.
9. Tape the straw to the top of the car with the balloon in the middle of the car and the end of the straw off the back.
10. Blow into the straw to blow up the balloon as big as you can, and then place the car on the floor and watch it zoom!

What's Happening?

When you let the air out of the balloon, it shoots out the back of the car. In the process, it pushes the balloon in the other direction with the same amount of force to make the balloon car zoom.

Super Spool Racer

This little racer is small enough to carry in your pocket.

DO IT!

Supplies

Empty thread spool, Rubber band, Paper clip, Washer, Tape, Pencil

1. Thread the paper clip onto the rubber band.
2. Push the rubber band through the hole in the middle of the spool and then through the washer.
3. Slide the pencil through the rubber band next to the washer.
4. Use tape to hold the paper clip in place on the other end of the spool.
5. Spin the pencil around until the rubber band is tight.
6. Lay the spool (with the pencil) on the ground and watch it go!

What's Happening?

The rubber band, which holds potential energy, untwists and causes the spool to spin and roll on the ground. The washers provide a smooth surface so that friction doesn't convert the motion energy into heat energy.

Totally Tubular Race Cars

Set up a drag race with your friends to find the fastest car!

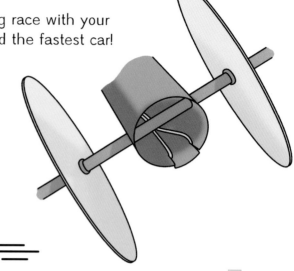

Supplies

Paper towel tube, 4 CDs or DVDs, 2 pencils, Rubber bands, Masking tape, Scissors, Glue, Hole punch

DO IT!

1. Use the hole punch to make holes in the paper towel tube exactly opposite each other on both ends. Make sure the holes line up across the tube opening and lengthwise so the wheels all sit on the ground and roll straight.
2. Slide pencils through the holes in the front and the back for axles, making sure the pencils spin freely in the holes.
3. Wrap several layers of masking tape around one end of a pencil, using enough tape that it will slide into the opening on a CD and not slide out.
4. Use a small amount of glue to make sure all of the CD wheels are secure.
5. Loop several rubber bands together to make a chain that is at least as long as the paper towel tube, and loop or tie one end of the chain to the back axle of the car.
6. On the other end, cut two slits about an inch apart on the bottom of the tube.
7. Feed the rubber band chain through the tube and hook the end of the chain onto the slits.
8. Make sure the rubber band chain is underneath the front axle, and then use a piece of tape to hold it in place.
9. Turn the back wheels to wind the rubber band tightly around the axle. When you can't wind the wheels anymore, let them go and watch the car zoom!

What's Happening?

Stretch out a rubber band and let it fly. The stretching adds energy to the rubber band, which is released when you let go and it goes flying with kinetic or motion energy.

The exact same thing happens inside the CD tube race car. Except in this case, the rubber band is attached to the axle of the car. To stretch the rubber band, you wind it around the axle. When it is released, instead of flying, the rubber band spins the axle and the race car zooms!

What If?

What if you make the tube shorter or longer? What else can you change to make your CD tube car move faster and farther?

Basic Paper Airplane

Many of the earliest flight scientists, from Leonardo da Vinci to the Wright Brothers, used paper models to design airplanes. Now you can make one too!

Supplies

Paper (8½ x 11 inches)

 **DO IT!**

For all of the steps in folding a paper airplane, make sure you crease each fold well by running your finger along the fold several times.

1. Fold the paper in half longways and then open it up again.

2. Fold the top right corner down so the top of the paper meets the first fold in the center, and then do the same on the left side. You should now have a folded triangle above a rectangle.

3. Fold the top side of the triangle to meet the first fold in the center of the paper.

4. Do the same on the left side, and then fold the paper in half longways along the center fold, so the folded parts are on the outside.

5. Lay the folded paper on its side, and then fold the long open edge of the top part so it meets the closed side (the center fold).

6. Turn the folded paper over and repeat the process, and then open the last fold to a right angle, creating the wings.

7. To fly the airplane, hold the center fold so the wings are on top, and then pull back your arm and throw the plane just slightly upward. How far does it fly?

What's Happening?

Paper airplanes, like real airplanes, are under four different forces. When you throw the airplane, you apply a forward moving force called thrust. You can give the airplane more thrust by throwing it harder. In a real airplane, the engines provide thrust.

Air pushing against the airplane as it moves is called drag. Drag works against thrust to slow down the airplane. Lift keeps the airplane up in the air. Air moving over and under the wings provides this upward force. The weight of the airplane, or gravity, pulls the airplane down toward the ground.

When designing a paper airplane, the goal is to provide the greatest lift with the smallest drag, so the airplane stays in the air for a long time and moves through the air quickly!

What If?

What if you adjust the folds on the airplane to increase the lift and decrease the drag? Can you design a paper airplane that flies faster or a greater distance?

Paper Glider

Can you build a glider that stays in the air longer than 30 seconds—the world record?

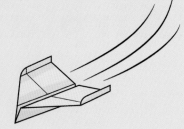

Supplies

Paper (8½ x 11 inches)

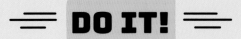 **DO IT!**

For all of the steps in folding a paper airplane, make sure you crease each fold well by running your finger along the fold several times.

1. Fold the paper in half longways and then open it up again.
2. Fold the top right corner down so the top of the paper meets the first fold in the center, then do the same on the left side. You should now have a folded triangle above a rectangle.
3. Fold the top half of the triangle down so the point meets the bottom, and then fold the triangle down along its bottom edge. The paper should now be a rectangle with the folded parts at the top.
4. Fold the top corners of the rectangle down to the center fold. Then fold the entire plane in half toward you, along the center fold so the folded parts are inside.
5. Create wings by folding each side out ½ inch from the center fold. This is where you will hold the plane.
6. Finally, fold up about ½ inch along the outside edge of each wing.
7. To fly the airplane, hold the center fold so the wings are on top and throw the plane almost straight up.

What's Happening?

A glider is designed to increase lift so that it stays in the air longer—even if it doesn't travel as quickly.

Straw Glider

This glider may not look like much, but it can fly farther than most paper airplanes.

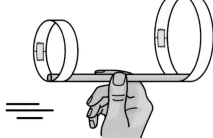

 **DO IT!**

Supplies

Straw, Paper, Ruler, Scissors, Tape

1. Cut a strip of paper 10 inches long and 1 inch wide.
2. Cut another strip 5 inches long and 1 inch wide, and then tape the strips into a hoop.
3. Tape a hoop to each end of the straw, making sure the straw is inside the hoops and the hoops are on the same side of the straw.
4. Hold the straw in the middle, with the hoops on top, and throw it like a spear. How long does the straw glider stay in the air? How far does it glide?

What's Happening?

This glider's hoops provide lift to keep it in the air, and with no wings, there's practically no drag.

Balloon Flinker

When an object floats and sinks at the same time, it's called a flinker.

DO IT!

Supplies

Helium balloon with a string or ribbon; Paper cup; Scissors; Small objects of different weights; Clock or stopwatch

1. Use the scissors to poke small holes on opposite sides of the cup near the top.
2. Thread the string from the helium balloon through both holes and tie the end back to the string above the cup. The cup should hang from the balloon like a hot-air-balloon basket.
3. Add small objects to the cup until the balloon can flink — or hang mid-air — for at least 30 seconds.

What's Happening?

A flinker equalizes the forces so that gravity pulls down just as much as the buoyant force pushes up. So the flinker just stays where it is, stuck in mid-air!

Hot-air Balloon

ADULT NEEDED

Use an ordinary toaster to turn a garbage bag into a hot-air balloon.

DO IT!

Supplies

Toaster, 2 pieces of poster board, Tape, Lightweight kitchen-size garbage bag

1. Unplug the toaster and clean out any crumbs, and then put the toaster on the floor and plug it back in.
2. Tape the poster board together to make a tube that fits around the toaster but does not touch it.
3. Turn on the toaster and place the poster board tube over it. Be careful, the toaster will get hot!
4. Slide the garbage bag over the tube and wait for the toaster to heat up the air in the bag. The bag will gradually inflate, lift up off the poster board, and fly up to the ceiling! If the bag tips over, put a couple pieces of tape on opposite sides of the bag to give weight and balance to the bottom of the bag. Don't forget to turn off the toaster after the hot-air balloon lifts off!

What's Happening?

As the toaster heats up the air in the bag, the air molecules move farther apart and push some of that air out of the bag. Soon, the air in the bag is less dense than the air in the rest of the room, and the bag begins to float. As the air cools, the bag falls back to the ground.

Sled Kite

A sled kite is the easiest to get up into the air and keep flying in even the lightest breeze.

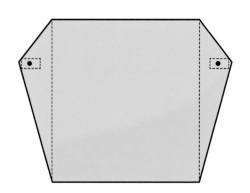

Supplies

White plastic garbage bag, Pen, Ruler, Scissors, Tape, Hole punch, 2 12-inch bamboo skewers or straws, Paper clip

1. Cut off the bottom of the garbage bag and down one side so you have a large single layer of white plastic.
2. Use the ruler and pen to draw a 12" x 9" rectangle in the center of the plastic, with the shorter side on top.
3. Measure 4 inches down from the top and draw a line across the rectangle so it extends exactly 4½ inches past the longer sides on each end.
4. Connect this point to the corners on that side of the rectangle, so you have a six-sided shape.
5. Cut out the shape.
6. Tape the skewers to the long sides of the rectangle, and then place a small piece of tape on both sides of the corners of the flaps outside of the skewers.
7. Use the hole punch to carefully put a hole in the tape, just in from the corner.
8. Cut a 36-inch piece of string, and tie one end of the string to each of the holes.
9. Tie one end of the rest of the string onto the stick and wrap all the string onto the stick.
10. Tie a paper clip onto the loose end of the string, and then hook the paper clip onto the loop of string tied to the holes. You're ready to fly your kite!

What's Happening?

To launch a kite, hold it up in the air and run as fast as you can as you let go of the kite. If you're lucky, a breeze will catch the kite and carry it up to the sky.

With a sled kite, the air inflates the kite, giving it a rounded shape like a wing. The air flowing over the kite has to go farther to get over the curve, so it moves faster than the air under the kite. Thanks to Bernoulli, we know that the still air has higher air pressure and pushes up harder than the fast-moving, low-pressure air pushes down. As long as there is wind or moving air, the kite will stay high in the sky!

What If?

What if you make your kite twice as big? Or even three times as big? Will it still fly?

Cool Diamond Kite

Did you know Benjamin Franklin tied a kite string to his foot while floating in a pond to see if the kite could pull him across the water?

Supplies

2 bamboo skewers, String, Tape, Scissors, Plastic bag, Stick, Paper clip

1. Lay the bamboo skewers in a T shape so the crosswise skewer is about ⅓ of the way from the top of the lengthwise skewer.

2. Tie the skewers together securely with string.

3. Cut open the plastic bag so you have a single layer, lay the skewers on top of the bag, and cut out a diamond shape slightly longer and wider than the skewers.

4. Use string or tape to securely attach the corners of the bag to the ends of the skewers.

5. Cut a piece of string 20 inches long and tie one end to the top of your kite and the other to the bottom of the kite.

6. Cut another piece of string 36 inches long and tie it to the bottom of the kite.

7. Cut six 6-inch strips from the rest of the plastic bag. Tie the strips onto the string several inches apart to make the tail of your kite.

8. Tie one end of the rest of the string onto the stick, and then wrap all the string onto the stick.

9. Tie a paper clip onto the loose end of the string.

10. Hook the paper clip onto the loop of string attached to the top and bottom of the kite. You are ready to fly your kite!

11. Take your kite outside in an open space, hopefully on a day with a good breeze. Never fly your kite during a thunderstorm or near electrical lines. Slowly unroll the string as the wind takes your kite up, up, and up!

What's Happening?

The key to keeping a kite in the air is the tail. Wind gives the kite lift, but it can also cause the kite to roll and turn. A tail adds weight to the bottom of the kite to keep it from rolling or spinning, which can tangle up the string or cause your kite to crash. Most kite flyers recommend a tail that is three to eight times longer than the length of the kite.

What If?

What if you use a long ribbon for a tail? What about more than one ribbon? What other materials or configurations can you use for a kite tail?

Paper Bag Kite

Have a blast with this easy-to-assemble flyer!

Supplies

Large brown paper grocery bag, 2 straws, String, Scissors, Tape, Glue, Stick, Paper clip, Paper streamer or tissue paper, Markers or crayons (optional)

═ DO IT! ═

1. Make a slit about 1 inch long on one end of a straw, then squeeze the straw and slide it into the other straw.
2. Use tape to secure the two straws together.
3. Cut the two short sides and one long side of the paper bag so you have a flap left on the bottom.
4. Fold the flap out and lay the straws where the flap meets the bag, centering the straws so there is at least an inch sticking out on either side of the bag.
5. Glue the straws in place, and then fold the flap into the bag and glue it down, as well.
6. Cut a length of string three times longer than the width of the paper bag.
7. Squeeze one end of the straw and use the scissors to snip a tiny triangle out of a side of the straw, near the middle.
8. Thread one end of the string through the hole and out the end of the straw and tie the string in place, and then use a piece of tape or some glue to hold it in place.
9. Repeat this process with the other end of the straw and the other end of the string.
10. Cut eight streamers from tissue paper or other lightweight material you might have handy. The streamers should be about three times longer than your kite.
11. Glue or tape two streamers inside each corner of the top of the bag.
12. Tie one end of the rest of the string onto the stick and wrap all the string onto the stick.
13. Tie a paper clip onto the loose end of the string, and hook the paper clip onto the loop of string attached to the straws. You're ready to fly your kite!
14. Take your kite outside in an open space, hopefully on a day with a good breeze. Slowly unroll the string as the wind takes your kite up, up, and up!

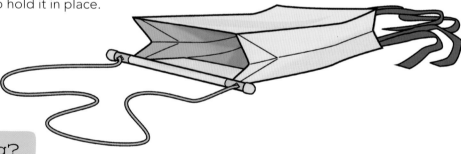

What's Happening?

As long as there is some wind, faster-moving air moves over the kite and slower-moving air moves inside and under the kite. Bernoulli's principle states that the slower-moving air pushes harder than the faster-moving air, giving your kite lift and keeping it in the air.

What If?

What if you use a paper lunch bag? Does the smaller bag fly more easily?

Perfect Parachute

Have you ever wondered how a parachute can allow someone to jump from a plane at astounding heights and land safely on the ground? Make a parachute yourself to figure it out!

Supplies

Large plastic garbage bag, Scissors, Ruler, String, Tape, Action figure or another toy with similar weight, Stopwatch, A friend to run the stopwatch

 DO IT!

1. Cut down one side of the garbage bag and open it up to make a large sheet of plastic.
2. Cut out a 24" x 24" square from the plastic, then cut four pieces of string, each 24 inches long.
3. Tape one string to each corner of the square.
4. Gather the other ends of the string and tie a knot at the end.
5. Use another piece of string and tape if needed to attach the action figure to the end of the four strings.
6. Find a high place to drop the parachute from, such as over a staircase or from the top of a jungle gym, and hold the parachute open so the action figure hangs down.
7. Drop the parachute and time how long it takes to reach the ground.
8. Remove the action figure and drop it from the same height without a parachute. What is the difference between the times with and without a parachute?

What's Happening?

Gravity pulls the parachute and action figure downward. At the beginning of the fall, the parachute expands and fills with air. As they fall, air continually pushes out the edges of the parachute and new air pushes in as everything moves downward.

The effect is air pushing upward on the parachute, called air resistance, which acts against gravity and slows the fall of the action figure. The force of air resistance increases as the parachute falls faster until it exactly equals gravity. From then on, the parachute and action figure will fall at a constant speed, called terminal velocity, until they reach the ground.

What If?

What if instead of an action figure you attach a raw egg? Can you drop the egg with a parachute so that it does not break?

Dragonfly Helicopter

The Chinese invented this toy thousands of years ago and called it the "bamboo dragonfly."

Supplies

Straw, Scissors, Cardstock or light cardboard like a cereal box, Stapler, Ruler

DO IT!

1. Cut two pieces of cardstock ¾ inch wide and 4 inches long.
2. Flatten one end of the straw and cut a ½-inch slit down the center.
3. Slide the two pieces of cardstock together into the slit and staple them to the straw.
4. Fold and crease the cardstock down and at an angle to make the propeller.
5. Open the blades of the propeller up so the two sides are straight out but slightly angled.
6. To launch the helicopter, hold the straw between your open hands with the propeller on top. Slide your hands in opposite directions to spin the straw and watch the helicopter take off!

What's Happening?

As a helicopter propeller moves through the air, the air underneath the wing pushes up more than the air on top pushes down. Unlike airplane wings, a propeller can hover.

Homemade Hovercraft

No need to search the skies for alien ships—you can build your own hovercraft!

Supplies

CD or DVD (that doesn't need to be used again), Pop top bottle top (from a sports drink bottle or dishwashing soap bottle), Craft glue, Balloon

DO IT!

1. Glue the bottle top onto the CD directly over the hole in the center.
2. Once the glue is dry, blow up the balloon.
3. Pinch the balloon closed with one hand while you use the other to stretch the opening over the bottle top.
4. Place the hovercraft on a flat surface, such as a hard floor.
5. Pull open the bottle top and let go of the balloon. Watch your hovercraft glide smoothly over the floor! How long does it glide before the balloon runs out of air?

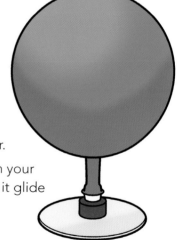

What's Happening?

Hovercrafts don't hover far off the ground, but they do move around easily with very little friction. In this experiment, the air from the balloon pushes down through the bottle top to create a thin layer of air between the hovercraft and the floor. This air eliminates almost all the friction between the floor and CD so it can glide around.

Fun with Friction

What material heats up the most from friction?

Supplies

Washcloth, Wire coat hanger, Wooden skewer, Plastic pen, Cardboard, Tape

=== DO IT! ===

1. Cut a piece of cardboard 8 inches long and 3 inches wide. Roll it up like a pencil and tape it together.
2. One at a time, hold the hanger, skewer, pen, and cardboard. Do they each feel cool or warm?
3. Hold the washcloth tightly around a straight part of the hanger and rub it at least 30 times. Feel the wire where you rubbed the cloth. Does it feel cool or warm?
4. Repeat this with the skewer, pen, and cardboard. Which material changed temperature the most?

What's Happening?

The amount of heat produced by friction depends on the materials and how hard they're pressed together. Even though the hanger is smooth, it gets hot because metals absorb heat easily. That's why we use metal pots and pans to cook.

Plastic and cardboard are insulators, so they do not hold onto the heat as well. All the materials gain some heat energy when the friction converts the energy of motion into heat.

Ball Bearings

What makes the wheels on a bicycle spin so fast? Ball bearings!

Supplies

Soup can, Jar lid that fits over the soup can, Pencil, Modeling clay, 12 marbles

=== DO IT! ===

1. Put a ball of modeling clay on each end of the pencil.
2. Lay the pencil across the middle of the jar lid and hold it in place with clay.
3. Push one end of the pencil to make the jar lid spin around on the soup can. How many times does it go around?
4. Remove the jar lid and put the marbles on top of the soup can.
5. Put the jar lid back on top of the marbles and spin the pencil and jar lid again. How many times does it go around now?

What's Happening?

Wheels spin around an axle. Without ball bearings, the wheel would rub against the axle, and sliding friction would convert all the motion energy into heat energy. The wheels would heat up and your toy would stop moving. With ball bearings between the wheel and axle, the ball bearings — like the marbles— roll around. Rolling friction is much smaller than sliding friction, so the pencil and jar spin more before friction slows everything down.

Rollin' with Friction

How can you reduce the effect of friction?

Supplies

Shoebox,
Balloon,
Scissors,
Straws, Tape,
Ruler

DO IT!

1. Cut a hole in one end of the box. Push the balloon through the hole, leaving the opening outside the box.
2. Blow up the balloon and hold the end closed. Place the box on the floor and let go of the balloon. Measure how far the box moves.
3. Try other surfaces, such as carpet and sidewalk. On which surface did the box slide the farthest?
4. Lay the straws side by side to make a 3-foot-long row.
5. Blow up the balloon and place the box on one end of the straw runway, then let it go. Measure how far the box moves. Does it move farther with the runway or without?

What's Happening?

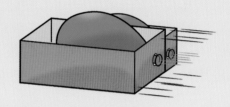

When two surfaces move against each other, there is sliding friction. Sliding friction converts motion energy into heat energy and slows things down. More force between the surfaces, and rough surfaces, cause more friction. The box slides farther on smooth surfaces than on rough surfaces.

When the box is on the straws, it creates rolling friction. Rolling friction is many times smaller than sliding friction, so the box moves farther before the rolling friction slows it down.

Phone Book Friction

Legend has it that if you interweave the pages of a phone book, it is impossible to pull apart!

Supplies

2 phone books,
Friend

DO IT!

1. Weave the pages of the books together by turning over one page at a time from alternating books. Keep going until you've weaved all the pages.
2. Have your friend grab the spine of one book as you grab the spine of the other. Pull as hard as you can. Can you pull the books apart?

What's Happening?

The force holding the books together is static friction. Static friction depends on the force between the two objects and the properties of the two materials in contact. Heavy objects with rough surfaces have more friction than light objects with smooth surfaces. When you weave together the pages of a book, the weight of the pages adds up. The pages also become bent at an angle, especially with thicker books. When you hold the spines to pull the books apart, you squeeze the pages together. All these factors create a LOT of force and make it nearly impossible to pull apart.

Sticky Rice

Can you lift a bottle of rice using just a pencil?

Supplies

Glass or plastic soda bottle, Rice, Funnel, Pencil

DO IT!

1. Funnel the rice into the bottle to the very top. Use the pencil to pack the rice down into the bottle, and add more rice to the top. Keep packing and adding rice until it is difficult to pull the pencil out of the rice.
2. Push the pencil down as far as you can, but leave enough of the pencil sticking out of the bottle to hold on to.
3. Hold the pencil and slowly pull it up. Can you lift the bottle of rice?

What's Happening?

When you first pour the rice into the bottle, there's a lot of space between the grains of rice. As the rice is packed into the bottle, this extra space is removed. When the pencil is pushed into the bottle, there is nowhere for the rice grains to go to make room for the pencil, so they push against the pencil. The rice pushing on the pencil provide enough friction force to prevent you from pulling the pencil out!

Science Friction

For something to slide, it must overcome static friction. How does weight affect this?

DO IT!

Supplies

Shoe, Rubber band, Scissors, Rocks, Ruler

1. Cut the rubber band into one long piece. Attach one end to the back of your shoe and put the shoe on a flat, smooth surface.
2. Pull the rubber band until the shoe is just about to move. Measure how far the rubber band stretches.
3. Place some rocks in the shoe. Pull the rubber band again until the shoe is just about to move and measure how far it stretches. How much longer did the rubber band get when you added weight to the shoe?

What's Happening?

To slide the shoe, you need to pull harder than the static friction that holds the shoe in place. Once the shoe slides, sliding friction takes over. Static friction is many times bigger than sliding friction. Once the shoe moves, it's easier to pull because the sliding friction pulls back with less force. The heavy shoe has more friction than the lighter shoe. More static friction means a bigger force is needed to move the shoe, and bigger forces stretch the rubber band longer.

A Penny for Your Bottle

Your challenge: Put a coin inside a bottle using just one finger.

Supplies

Bottle, Index card, Coin (must fit through the bottle opening)

DO IT!

1. Place the index card on top of the bottle.
2. Place the coin on top of the card over the bottle opening. Check all sides to make sure it's right in the center.
3. Now put the coin inside the bottle using just one finger. Can you do it without reading ahead?

What's Happening?

Inertia is the tendency for an object, like the coin, to stay put until a force acts on it. The only thing keeping the coin from going in the bottle is the card. If you apply a force to the card, and only the card, to remove it from under the coin, the coin will fall into the bottle. Just use your finger to quickly flick the card straight out from under the coin. Make sure the card moves straight and doesn't flip to push the coin up and away from the bottle.

Change-ing Tower

Your next challenge: Remove the bottom level of a coin tower without toppling it.

Supplies

10 coins, Plastic knife, Tabletop

DO IT!

1. Stack the coins to make a small, straight tower.
2. Now remove the bottom coin from the tower using only the knife without knocking over or moving the rest of the tower. Can you do it without reading ahead?

What's Happening?

To solve the challenge, hold the tip of the plastic knife flat on the table. Slide the knife quickly and smoothly so that you just kick the bottom coin out from under the tower. The key is to move fast and not hesitate. Because you are only applying a force to the bottom coin, that's the only coin that will move. The inertia, or tendency to stay at rest, of the other coins in the tower will hold it in place.

What If?

What if you use more or fewer coins? What if you use coins of different sizes or weights? Does this make it harder or easier to remove the bottom coin?

Don't Drop This Egg

You'll have "egg drop" soup if you don't do this one right!

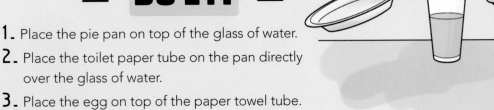

Supplies

Egg (raw if you dare, but hard-boiled works too), Toilet paper tube, Pie plate, Glass of water

DO IT!

1. Place the pie pan on top of the glass of water.
2. Place the toilet paper tube on the pan directly over the glass of water.
3. Place the egg on top of the paper towel tube.
4. Now get the egg into the glass of water with just one hand. Can you do it without reading ahead?

What's Happening?

Because of inertia, the egg will stay where it is unless a force acts on it. To make it work, you just need to remove the pan and tube so the egg falls straight down into the glass. To do this, just give the pan a quick chop sideways. It will fly off the glass. The edge of the pan will hook the tube so that it gets out of the way, as well. Without the tube to hold it up, gravity will pull the egg down into the glass.

Streak of Beads

These beads keep going and going, with some surprising effects.

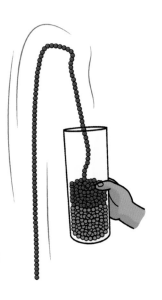

Supplies

4 strings of round plastic beads, Scissors, Glue gun, Jar that will hold the beads

DO IT!

1. Make one cut to each string of beads.
2. Glue the end of one string of beads to the next, until you have one long chain of beads.
3. Feed one end of the chain into the jar carefully so there are no tangles or knots.
4. Once the beads are in the jar, hold on to the end of the chain at the top.
5. Hold the jar up high and let go of the end of the chain of beads to watch them streak out!

What's Happening?

As soon as you let go of the end of the chain of beads, gravity pulls them downward. The beads at the bottom pull on the ones above, and once they start moving, the beads will keep moving until they hit the floor because of inertia. Inertia is the tendency of an object to keep moving at the same speed and in the same direction until a force acts on it. These beads keep moving, and pulling along the beads behind them, until the floor applies a force to stop them.

Balancing Stick

Can you make a stick stand on its end?

DO IT!

Supplies

Yardstick,
Clay

1. Cup your hand and put the end of the stick on your palm. Let go of the stick with your other hand. Are you able to keep the stick upright?
2. Place a fist-sized lump of clay around the stick, about 8 inches from one end.
3. Try to balance the stick in the same way with the clay end up high. Now try to balance it with the clay end down low. Which situation is easiest to balance the stick?

What's Happening?

The tendency of an object to spin is called rotational inertia. It depends on the amount of mass and how far the mass is from the pivot point. In this case, the pivot point is the end of the stick in the palm of your hand. When the clay is up high, far from the pivot point, the stick has more rotational inertia than when it is down low. This means the stick turns more slowly when the clay is high, and tips over easier when it is low.

Buckets of Dryness

Amaze your friends by swinging water over your head and staying completely dry!

DO IT!

Supplies

Bucket, Water,
Outdoor space

1. Fill the bucket with a few inches of water, making sure it's not too heavy and you can lift it easily.
2. Hold the bucket in front of your body and swing it back and forth, getting a little faster each time.
3. When you feel confident, swing the bucket all the way around over your head. Move the bucket fast and do not slow down until you reach the bottom of the swing. After some practice, try swinging the bucket in a circle several times without stopping.

What's Happening?

The water stays in the bucket because of inertia. Inertia is the tendency of a moving object to keep moving in a straight line. When you swing the bucket back and forth, that straight line is to the left or the right. But the bucket pulls the water into a curved path using centripetal force.

When you swing the bucket over your head, the same thing happens. The inertia of the water is sideways, but the bucket pulls it into a circle. If the inertia of the water is greater than gravity, you will stay dry!

Sticky Balloons

You might want to get several balloons and have a party, because this experiment will really get you charged up about static electricity!

Supplies

Balloons, Your hair or a wool sweater, Mirror, Wall

 **DO IT!**

1. Take a balloon and rub it on your hair or a wool sweater for at least 15 seconds.
2. Look in the mirror and hold the balloon a few inches from your head. Your hair should jump up and reach for the balloon.
3. Give the balloon a few more rubs on your head and then stick it on the wall. It should hang right there for quite a while: up to 30 minutes on a very dry day!

What's Happening?

Electrons are the key to electricity! Electrons are tiny, negatively charged parts of the atom that swarm and spin around the central, positively charged nucleus. For some materials called conductors (like most metals), these electrons can easily move from one atom to another. Other materials are called insulators because they hold onto their electrons more tightly, such as plastics, hair, and fur. The electricity that we use to power our appliances and electronics is just a flow of electrons through a wire. But static electricity involves electrons that are stuck in one place. We can create a static charge by rubbing together two insulators, such as a balloon and your hair.

Friction moves the electrons from one insulator to another, leaving the balloon negatively charged (it gained some electrons) and your hair positively charged (because it lost electrons). Opposites attract and likes repel. So, when the negatively charged balloon is placed near your positively charged hair, they will attract each other, causing your hair to stand up.

You can even have a charged object pull toward a neutral object like a wall. The wall is made of atoms just like everything else, and placing the balloon on the wall will polarize or move more positive charges toward the balloon and negative charges away, so that there is a pull between the negative balloon and the positive charges in the wall that holds the balloon in place.

What If?

What if you use something else to charge up your balloon? Try blankets and fabrics of different types, such as wool, cotton, nylon, and silk. You can even try furry pets! How about metal, plastic, wood, or other hard surfaces?

Bending Water

Use the power of static electricity to move a stream of running water.

Supplies

Plastic comb,
Your hair,
Water faucet

DO IT!

1. Turn on the faucet and adjust the flow until there's just a thin stream of water flowing.
2. Comb your hair at least 10 times with the plastic comb.
3. Slowly bring the comb near the stream of flowing water without touching the water. The water should bend its direction of flow toward the comb! Move the comb around and watch what happens to the water.

What's Happening?

When you comb your hair, you not only get a sharp-looking hairdo, you also scrape electrons off your hair and onto the comb, giving it a negative charge. The water has both negative and positive charges. When you hold the comb near the stream of water, the positive charges in the water are attracted to the negative charges on the comb, and the stream of water bends.

Dancing Balloons

This experiment is truly repulsive! The negativity of these balloons keeps them from ever coming together.

Supplies

2 balloons, 2 pieces of string at least 2 feet long, Your hair or a wool sweater

DO IT!

1. Blow up both balloons.
2. Tie a string to the end of each balloon. If you'd like, draw faces on your balloons with a marker.
3. Rub the balloons on your head or a wool sweater to charge them with electrons.
4. Hold the ends of the strings together so the balloons hang down together, and watch the fun! The charged balloons should dance around each other without touching.

What's Happening?

Rubbing the balloons on your head scrapes electrons off your hair and onto the balloons. This leaves your head with a slightly positive charge and the balloons both with a negative charge. Like charges repel. Because the balloons are both negatively charged, they will dance around each other but never touch — at least not until the electrons have escaped into the air.

Levitating Tinsel

Make something fly with the
magical power of static electricity!

Supplies

**Seven 6-inch
strands of tinsel,
Scissors, Balloon,
Your head**

DO IT!

1. Lay out six pieces of tinsel together in a long bundle.
2. Cut two small pieces from the extra piece of tinsel and tie both ends of the tinsel bundle together.
3. Charge up a balloon by rubbing it on your hair.
4. Hold the tinsel above the balloon and drop it onto the balloon. What happens?

What's Happening?

When you rub the balloon on your hair, electrons are scraped off and transferred to the balloon, and the balloon is negatively charged. At first, the tinsel has no charge. When you drop it onto the balloon, some of those electrons are transferred to the tinsel. Now both the balloon and the tinsel are negatively charged! Objects with the same charge repel each other. The tinsel hovers above the balloon with gravity pulling it down, and the repelling electrostatic force of the electrons pushing it up. Eventually, the extra electrons on the tinsel escape into the air, but for a few seconds, it can defy gravity!

Spark Zapper

Static electricity can be shocking! Use this tool
to make your own sparks whenever you want.

Supplies

**Metal pie tin, Styrofoam
plate, Styrofoam cup,
Scissors, Masking tape,
Your head**

DO IT!

1. Tape the Styrofoam cup to the center of the pie tin.
2. Rub the Styrofoam plate all over your head for five seconds.
3. Put the plate down on the table, upside down.
4. Pick up the pie tin by the cup and drop it onto the plate.
5. Touch the edge of the pie tin. You will get zapped by a spark!

What's Happening?

When you rub the Styrofoam plate on your hair, you're scraping negative electrons off your head and onto the plate. The pie tin has a bunch of free electrons that can move around. When you put the pie tin on the foam plate, those free electrons are repelled by the extra electrons on the Styrofoam and try to get away. As soon as you put your finger near the pie tin, they jump onto your finger. Zap!

Salt & Pepper Pick-up

Use the force of static electricity to separate salt from pepper.

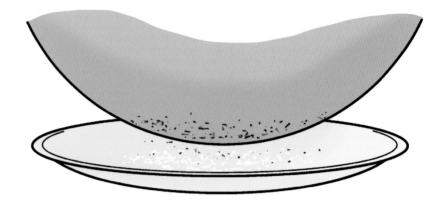

Supplies

Salt, Pepper, Paper plate, Spoon, Balloon, Your hair or a wool sweater

1. Pour 1 teaspoon of salt and 1 teaspoon of pepper on the paper plate. Use the spoon to mix them up so you have a pile in the center of the plate.
2. Blow up the balloon and tie off the end.
3. Rub the balloon on your hair or a wool sweater to charge it up with electrons.
4. Hold the balloon about an inch above the salt and pepper mixture and watch what happens! You should see the pepper jump off the plate and onto the balloon, leaving the salt behind.

What's Happening?

There are two reasons the pepper sticks to the balloon and the salt does not. First, the pepper polarizes much easier than the salt. That's because its electrons move mostly to one side of the pepper flake, leaving one end positive and the other with a negative charge. The positive end is attracted to the negative balloon. Salt does not polarize quite as much, so it doesn't feel as much of a pull. However, it will jump up on the balloon if you hold it very close to the plate. Also, the pepper flakes are much lighter than the salt crystals. So even if the salt does jump up onto the balloon, it's too heavy to stay and it falls back down.

You will also see some of the pepper and salt jump up to the balloon and then fly off. This is because it grabbed an electron off the balloon and suddenly became negatively charged – just like the balloon. The like charges repel, throwing the tiny particle away.

What If?

What if you try to separate other mixtures? Try sugar and cinnamon and any other mixtures you can make from the spice cabinet.

Gelatin Pick-up

Build tiny towers of gelatin powder with static electricity!

DO IT!

1. Pour 1 tablespoon of gelatin in the center of the plate.
2. Blow up the balloon and tie off the end.
3. Rub the balloon on your hair to charge it up with electrons.
4. Hold the balloon just above the plate but not touching the pile of gelatin.
5. Slowly pull the balloon up. You should see the gelatin form tiny towers as it reaches up toward the balloon!

What's Happening?

When the balloon is held near the gelatin particles, they become polarized. Electrons move mostly to one side of the gelatin particle, leaving one end positive and the other with a negative charge. The positive end of the particle is attracted to the negative balloon. As the balloon moves away from the plate, the gelatin particles form a chain with the negative ends attached to the positive ends. These chains look like tiny towers on the plate of gelatin powder. When the balloon moves too far away, the gelatin is no longer polarized and the towers collapse.

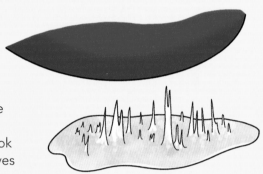

Static Slime

Can you stop slime in mid-flow? You sure can, with the help of static electricity!

DO IT!

1. Pour ¼ cup of oil into one of the cups. Mix in 3 to 4 tablespoons of cornstarch with the spoon until the liquid looks like thin gravy.
2. Blow up the balloon and rub it on your hair to charge it.
3. Pour the mixture from one cup into the other while holding your charged balloon near the flow of liquid. The liquid should stop flowing, and you might even see solid-looking chunks jump onto the balloon!

What's Happening?

When the cornstarch particles are in the electric field caused by the charged-up balloon, they link up like a net, which slows down the flow of the oil. As soon as you remove the electric field, the oil flows normally.

Sticky Statics

Electric charges cause all sorts of objects to attract and repel—even tape!

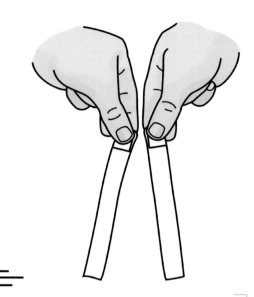

Supplies

A flat, smooth surface (a binder cover or countertop); Clear plastic tape; Scissors (optional)

 **DO IT!**

1. Place a 10-inch-long piece of tape onto the flat, smooth surface. This is the base tape.
2. Cut a 4-inch-long piece of tape and fold over a small amount on one end to make a handle.
3. Place the piece on top of the base tape.
4. Make another 4-inch piece in the same way and add it to the base tape.
5. Use the handle on the two smaller tapes and pull them off the base tape.
6. Hold these tapes so that they hang near each other. Do the tapes repel or attract? Try holding the tapes in different ways: non-sticky to non-sticky side, sticky to non-sticky side, and sticky to sticky side. Does the way you hold the tape affect whether they attract or repel?
7. One at a time, gently rub your fingers over both sides of the tapes. Bring them together again. Do they act differently now?
8. Stick the two pieces of tape together (non-sticky to sticky side) so that you have a double-thick piece of tape. Run your fingers over the tape to remove any leftover charges.
9. Pull the two pieces of tape apart by their handles. Hold the tapes so that they hang near each other. Do the tapes repel or attract? Try all the different combinations of holding the tapes as above.

What's Happening?

In the first part of the experiment, you pulled two separate pieces of tape off the base tape. Pulling the tapes off the base tape charged the tapes in the same way. Because they have like charges, they will repel each other, no matter how you hold them.

However, in the second part of the experiment, you pulled the tapes apart from each other. This left one tape with a positive charge and the other with a negative charge. The different-charged tapes attracted each other.

What If?

What if you use your charged tape to see if other household objects have a charge? Try holding a charged tape near a TV or computer monitor (when they are turned on), refrigerator, cell phone, lamp, or any other object you think might be charged.

Soda Can Electroscope

Make your own electroscope so you can immediately detect an electric charge!

Supplies

Empty soda can, Masking tape, Styrofoam cup, Aluminum foil, Scissors, Balloon, Your hair or wool sweater

 **DO IT!**

1. Pull the tab of the can out so that it's perpendicular to the top of the can.
2. Turn the Styrofoam cup upside down and tape the can on top, so it lies sideways on the bottom of the cup and the tab on the can is vertical.
3. Cut two strips of aluminum foil about 2 inches long and ¼ inch wide.
4. Make a hook on the end of each strip, and use the hook to hang the strips from the tab of the can. The strips should hang right next to each other. Your electroscope is now ready to use!
5. Charge up a balloon by rubbing it on your hair or a wool sweater for several seconds.
6. Hold the balloon close to, but not touching, the soda can. What happens to the foil strips as the balloon gets closer to the can? What happens as you move it away?
7. Touch the charged balloon to the soda can. What happens to the foil strips when you touch the can? What happens when you take the balloon away?
8. Touch the soda can with your hand and observe what happens to the strips.

What's Happening?

When you move the charged balloon close to the can but don't touch it, the electroscope becomes charged by induction. The negative balloon repels the negative electrons to the other side of the can, so that one side is negatively charged and the other is positive. The foil strips are next to each other, so they will have a like charge and repel each other or move apart. When you move the balloon away, the charges spread out on the can and the foil strips hang down again.

When the charged balloon touches the electroscope, the can is charged by conduction. The extra electrons on the balloon move over to the can. The whole can is negatively charged, including the foil strips, so they repel each other. However, when you move the balloon away, the electroscope is still charged and the foil strips stay separated. When you touch the can with your hand, you ground the electroscope so that the extra electrons leave through your finger.

Magnetic Compass

Make a compass so you'll always know
which direction you're headed!

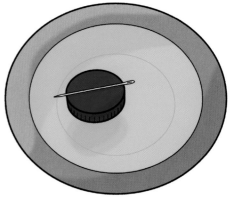

Supplies

**Small bowl of water, Sewing needle, Magnet, Plastic bottle
top, Tape, Compass or smartphone, Marker**

DO IT!

1. Magnetize the needle by rubbing it at least 50 times with one end of the magnet (the north end if it is labeled). Make sure you rub the needle in only one direction and lift the magnet off the needle each time.

2. Use a small piece of tape to secure the needle to the top of the bottle cap.

3. Float the bottle cap, with the needle on top, in the water. The needle will automatically turn to point north!

4. Use the compass or a smartphone with a compass app to figure out which end of the needle is pointing north, then use the marker to mark "N" near the north side of the bottle cap. Use your compass to figure out which direction the front door faces, which directions the street you live on runs, and which direction you go to get to school.

What's Happening?

Earth is a giant magnet! A compass is just a magnet that is free to move so it can align with the Earth's magnetic field. The bowl of water provides a low friction surface for the needle to float on and turn freely. Exposing the iron in the needle to the strong magnetic field in the magnet lines up the spin of the electrons in the needle's iron atoms, which then creates a magnetic field in the needle. Over time, the spinning electrons will fall out of line. You will then need to "recharge" your compass needle each time you use it.

What If?

What if you use a paper clip or nail instead of a needle? What if you hung the needle by a thread inside a jar so you can carry your compass around without spilling water? How else can you improve the design of this compass?

Nailed It Electromagnet

Unlike refrigerator magnets, which are always on, electromagnets only work when connected to a source of electricity.

Supplies

Long iron nail, Magnet wire (with an enamel coating), D battery, Electrical tape, Scissors, 12 small paper clips

What's Happening?

The coiled wire around the nail is called a solenoid. When electric current runs through the solenoid, it creates a magnetic field inside the metal coils. Iron has atoms that become magnetized in a magnetic field, which makes your electromagnet stronger.

ADULT NEEDED

DO IT!

1. Wrap the wire around the nail 20 times, leaving 6 inches of wire on each side.
2. With scissors, remove 1 inch of the plastic coating from both ends of the wire.
3. Tape each piece of exposed wire to one end of the battery. You've made an electromagnet! Hold it over a pile of paper clips. How many paper clips stick to your electromagnet? Make sure to disconnect the wires from the battery when you are done experimenting, but be careful, as the wires can get hot.

Floating Paper Clip

Defy gravity by levitating a paper clip in mid-air!

DO IT!

Supplies

Strong magnet, Paper clip, Thread, Scissors, Tall glass, Screwdriver, Tape, Test materials: penny, paper, cloth, etc.

1. Place the magnet on the end of the screwdriver, and then balance the screwdriver across the glass, so the magnet hangs 3 inches out from the edge of the glass.
2. Cut 12 inches of thread and tie it to the paper clip. Stick the paper clip to the magnet.
3. Slowly pull the thread downward until you pull the paper clip off the magnet and it floats a centimeter or two from the magnet.
4. Tape the thread down firmly so the paper clip stays put. Now you can test what materials block the magnetic field.
5. Place a penny between the paper clip and the magnet without touching the paper clip. What happens? Repeat the process for the other test materials. Which materials block the magnetic field and make the paper clip fall?

What's Happening?

Magnetic forces happen when the electrons spinning around atoms line up. This happens easier in some materials, like iron or nickel, than it does in other materials, like plastic or wood. When the paper clip touches the magnet, it becomes magnetized. The force between the magnet and paper clip keep it magnetized. The paper clip is caught between the upward force from the magnet and the downward force from the thread and gravity.

Magnet Gun

Can you hit a target with the power of magnets?

Supplies

2 neodymium magnets, 3 steel ball bearings, Ruler with a groove in the middle, Strong tape, Scissors, Table

Gauss: a unit of magnetic induction

DO IT!

1. Place two ball bearings at the end of the ruler. Tape one magnet next to the balls.
2. Slide the ruler so the ball and magnet are at the edge of the table. Trim extra tape off the magnet.
3. Roll another ball along the ruler toward the magnet. The ball on the end will shoot out!
4. Roll the ball at different speeds and from different distances. What happens?

What's Happening?

When the ball rolls toward the magnet, it speeds up because the magnet is pulling on it. As it accelerates, it gains kinetic energy. When the first ball hits the magnet, that energy is transferred to the magnet and the balls. The ball at the end shoots off with almost the same kinetic energy that the first ball had when it hit the magnet. Some of the energy is lost to sound and heat, but most is transferred to the ball at the end.

Electromagnetic Train

Make a train that zooms! **ADULT NEEDED**

DO IT!

1. Make two stacks of three neodymium batteries. Point the stacks toward each other so that they repel. Place each stack on either end of the battery.
2. Tape one end of the wire to the end of the dowel. Tightly wrap wire around 4 inches of the dowel. Slide the coil off.
3. Stretch the coils apart so that each loop does not touch.
4. Place the battery-magnet train into the coil. Watch it zoom to the other end! If your train doesn't move, flip it around or turn over the stack of magnets on one end.

Supplies

Copper wire (16 gauge, uncoated), AAA battery, 6 neodymium magnets slightly bigger than the battery, Dowel, Tape

What's Happening?

When you place your train into the coil, it creates an electric circuit. Electricity travels from one end of the battery, through the magnet into the wire, where it travels around the battery and back in through the magnet on the other end. The electricity creates its own magnetic field. The magnets on the battery are lined up so that the magnetic field in the wire pushes the train through the coil.

Minute Motor

This electric motor is so simple, it can be put together in about a minute!

Supplies

AA battery, Screw (that will stick to a magnet), Neodymium battery, Insulated wire, Electrical tape, Scissors

ADULT NEEDED  **DO IT!**

1. Remove some of the plastic insulation from each end of the wire.
2. Tape one end of the wire to the negative end of the battery.
3. Place the magnet on the flat end of the screw, and then put the pointed end of the screw on the positive end of the battery.
4. Hold the battery so the screw and magnet hang downward.
5. Touch the loose end of the wire to the magnet and watch the screw spin around!

What's Happening?

When the end of the loose wire touches the magnet, you give the electric current in the battery a path to follow. The current flows out of the battery, through the wire, into the magnet, through the screw, and back to the battery. Any object with a current flowing through it in a magnetic field is pushed on by the Lorentz force, which causes the screw to spin around.

Magnetic Fruit

Can magnets stick to food?

DO IT!

Supplies

Large toothpick, Thread, Scissors, Tape, Fruit, Strong magnet, Ruler

1. Tape a ruler to a countertop with 6 inches hanging over the edge.
2. Cut an 18-inch piece of thread. Tape it to the ruler longways down the ruler.
3. Tie the middle of the toothpick to the other end of the string.
4. Slide a grape onto each end of the toothpick so the toothpick is balanced. Let the grapes hang until they stop turning.
5. Slowly move the magnet toward the grape. Does the grape move? Does it move toward or away from the magnet? Try other grape-sized pieces of fruit. Do they move near the magnet?

What's Happening?

The reason why the fruits moved slowly away from the strong magnet is because of a weak magnetism that repels objects, known as diamagnetism. When some non-metals are in an electric field, the electrons spinning in the atom line up opposite of the magnetic field in the magnet, which creates a repelling force so weak that you can only see it when you hang the fruit on a string. If you put the grape on a table near a magnet, it won't move at all.

This Battery Is a Lemon

Create your own electricity with fruit!

Supplies

6 lemons, 6 nails or large paper clips, Heavy copper wire (with or without plastic coating), Wire cutters or heavy scissors, 1 LED or light bulb from holiday lights (with wires attached), Electrical tape

DO IT!

1. Cut the copper wire into six 8-inch lengths and two 10-inch lengths. Cut off about an inch of the plastic insulation from both ends of each wire.

2. Squeeze and roll the lemons on the table so they are good and juicy on the inside without breaking the skin.

3. Stick a nail about halfway in each of the lemons.

4. Connect the lemons in a row with the short copper wires.

5. Stick the ends of the copper wire into the lemon close to the nail, but not touching.

6. Connect a long wire to each wire or lead on the light bulb using electrical tape.

7. Stick the other ends of the copper wire into a lemon on each end of the row. Watch the light bulb light up! If you are using an LED and it doesn't light up, just switch the leg of the LED that each wire is attached to so the electricity flows in the right direction to light the bulb.

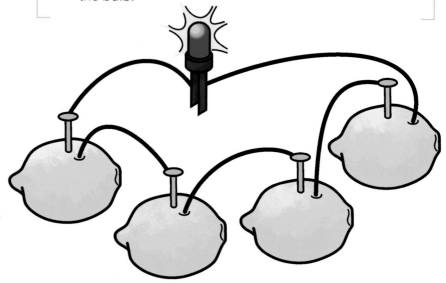

What's Happening?

Usually, your lights would be plugged into an electrical socket or would be powered by a battery, right? Batteries are made of two different metals and an acid. In this case, the lemon provides the acid. The nail and copper wire are the two different metals. The nail and wire are electrodes, where the electricity enters and leaves the battery. Electrons flow from the nail into the lemon juice acid to the copper wire, and then to the next lemon, gathering more and more electrons until there are enough to light up the bulb!

What If?

What if you use other fruit in your battery? Try other acidic fruits and vegetables, such as oranges, limes, tomatoes, and potatoes, and see what happens.

Holiday Light Circuits

Why do some holiday lights go out when one bulb goes out, but other lights stay lit?

ADULT NEEDED

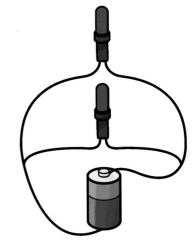

Supplies

Strand of holiday lights, Scissors, D battery, Electrical tape

DO IT!

1. Cut two lights off the strand, making sure each light has two long wires attached.
2. Remove an inch of plastic coating from the end of each wire.

Make a Series Circuit

1. Twist one light's wire to the other light's wire to attach them in a row. Tape them together.
2. Tape the wires at both ends of the lights to opposite ends of the battery. Do the bulbs light up? How bright are they? What happens if you take a bulb out?

Make a Parallel Circuit

1. Cut two extra pieces of wire, about 4 inches long, from the strand of lights.
2. Remove an inch of plastic coating from the end of each wire. Twist one light's wires to the other light's wires to create a circle.
3. Attach an extra wire where the wires from the light connect. Tape the wires together.
4. Touch the loose ends of the extra wires to opposite ends of the battery. Do the bulbs light up? How bright are they? What happens if you take a bulb out?

What's Happening?

For electrical current to light up a light bulb, it must have a complete circuit that connects from one end of a battery back to the other end. Both the series and parallel circuits make at least one loop for the electrical current to flow through. In a series circuit, there is one big loop for the current to flow through. The current flows through both lights in the circuit and the bulbs light brightly. If you take one bulb out, the loop is broken so the current stops flowing and the bulb that is left does not light up.

In a parallel circuit, there are two connected loops. Half the current goes through one light bulb and half goes through the other. Both bulbs light, but are half as bright as the bulbs in the series circuit. When one bulb is removed, there is still a path for the current and the other light bulb stays lit.

While light bulbs in a series circuit burn brighter, one burned-out light will make the whole strand of lights go out. In a parallel circuit, one burned-out light bulb does not take out all the lights in the strand.

Gassy Water

Break apart water atoms to make hydrogen gas and oxygen gas!

ADULT NEEDED

Supplies

Water, Salt, Measuring spoons, 2 cups, Clear glass, 2 lead pencils sharpened on both ends, two 8-inch lengths of plastic-coated copper wire, Scissors, 9-volt battery, Electrical tape, Outdoor space

= DO IT! =

1. Do this experiment outdoors. In one cup, mix ¾ tablespoons of salt into 1 cup of water to make a 5% saltwater solution.

2. In the other cup, mix 1½ tablespoons of salt with 1 cup of water to make a 10% saltwater solution. Label each cup.

3. Remove 1 inch of plastic coating from each end of both pieces of copper wire.

4. Wrap the end of one wire around the end of a pencil, making sure the wire touches the black graphite in the pencil.

5. Tape the wire in place, and do the same with the other pencil and wire.

6. Wrap the loose ends of the two wires around the leads on the battery: one on the positive end and one on the negative. Tape the wires in place.

7. Fill the glass halfway with water, and place the pencils in the glass. After several seconds, bubbles should cover the ends of the pencil. The bubbles on the pencil on the negative lead of the battery are hydrogen, and the other lead is oxygen.

8. Take the pencils out of the glass and empty the water.

9. Pour in the 5% saltwater solution and put the pencils back in. What happens? Repeat the experiment with the 10% saltwater solution. Which liquid created the most bubbles?

What's Happening?

On the pencil connected to the positive lead of the battery, water is oxidized. The water is broken into oxygen gas (O_2) and charged hydrogen ions. On the pencil connected to the negative lead of the battery, water is broken into hydrogen gas (H_2) and hydroxide ions. There are a lot more hydrogen bubbles on the positive lead than there are oxygen bubbles on the negative. Water (H_2O) has twice as many hydrogen atoms as oxygen. This means it releases twice as much hydrogen gas.

Salt is an electrolyte and helps the water conduct electricity more easily so more energy is available to break up the water molecule quicker. Once you add salt to the solution, the gas bubbles on the anode aren't just oxygen, but also contain some chlorine from the salt.

Homopolar Motor

How many motors do you have in your house? Refrigerators, blenders, computers, and toys that move all have motors. Can you make your own electric motor?

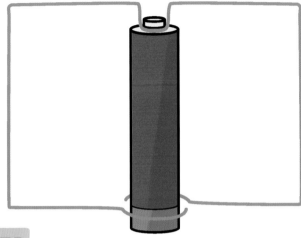

Supplies

AA battery, Neodymium magnet, Copper wire (16 gauge, uncoated), Pliers, Wire cutters

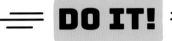 **DO IT!**

1. Cut off a 10-inch piece of copper wire.
2. Bend the wire into a square that is even on both sides, with a small dip at the top.
3. Curve the bottoms of the wire in opposite directions, making sure they touch the magnet but do NOT touch each other.
4. Put the magnet on the flat end of the battery.
5. Slide the wire onto the battery and magnet so the point at the top touches the bump on the top of the battery, and the curves at the bottom wrap around the magnet. As soon as the wire is in place, it will spin around! If the motor doesn't work, try turning the magnets upside down. If that doesn't work, try a fresh battery. Also make sure the wire is not getting stuck to the magnet or battery, and that the bottom of the wire is touching the magnet only.

What's Happening?

When you put the wire onto the battery and motor, an electric current flows through the wire, down to the magnet, and back to the battery on both sides. There is also a strong magnetic field from the magnets. Whenever there is an electrical current in a magnetic field, the wire carrying the current feels the Lorentz force, that is at a right angle to both the current and the magnetic field. The Lorentz force pushes the wire so that it spins around the battery.

What If?

What if you bend the wire into other shapes that spin around? Just make sure the shape is symmetrical so it doesn't fall off the battery when it spins around.

Electromagnetic Motor

This electric motor harnesses the power of a magnetic force to make it go!

ADULT NEEDED

Supplies

D or C battery, 2 large safety pins, Electrical tape, Magnet wire (wire with an enamel coating), Scissors, Strong magnet, Marker or other round object about ½ to 1 inch in diameter, Sandpaper

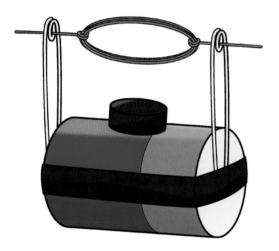

⇒ DO IT! ⇒

1. Tape the top of a safety pin to each end of the battery so that the bottom ends are pointing straight up in the same direction.

2. Wrap the magnet wire tightly around the marker 15 times.

3. Leave a 2-inch length of wire on each side of the loops.

4. Slide the loops off the marker and wrap the end pieces tightly around either side of the loop several times to hold the loop together. The rest of the end pieces should stick straight out from opposite sides of the loop.

5. Use the sandpaper to remove all the enamel coating from the end piece on one side of the loop. Then use the sandpaper to remove the enamel from just one side of the end piece on the other side of the loop.

6. Stick the end pieces of the loop through the holes at the bottom of the safety pins so the loop is now suspended over the battery.

7. Place the magnet on the battery, directly below the center of the loop. Watch the loop spin around!

What's Happening?

An electric motor uses the attracting and repelling properties of magnets to change electromagnetic energy into motion energy. This motor has two magnets: the strong magnet you placed on top of the battery and the electromagnet you created from the magnet wire. When electrons, in the form of electrical current from the battery, pass through the wire, it creates a weak magnetic field. By wrapping the wire several times into a loop, the magnetic field is stronger. The magnetic force from the strong magnet pushes and pulls on the loops of the electromagnet, causing it to spin around.

What If?

What if you use more or fewer loops in the electromagnet? What if you change the shape from a circle to a square or triangle? What if you make bigger loops? What is the biggest motor you can make?

Index